Chapter 7   Know Your Child
Chapter 8 Enhancing Your Child's Learning Ability
Chapter 9 How Marriage Impacts Fathering
Chapter 10 Values You Should Impart To Your Children
Chapter 11 Skills You Should Teach Your children
Chapter 12 How Fathering Affects Children's Career Choices
Chapter 13 Imparting Sexuality Education To Your Children
Chapter 14 The Divorced Father
Chapter 15 Preparing Your Children For Marriage
Chapter 16 Challenges of Youths in the 21st Century
About the author
Sample chapter of my new book
Other books by this author
Connect with the Author
Reading Group Discussion Guide

PREFACE

Essentially, fatherhood is the state of siring a child and providing for the needs of the child. It involves catering for the material, physical, spiritual, social and emotional needs of the child till the child is of age.

For many men, their most important obligation to their children is providing for their material needs. While not diminishing the importance of this role, other very important aspects of fathering like nurturing and mentoring are often ignored.

Men do not take to fathering by intuition; it is most often a learned act. Men, unlike women do not have biological experiences comparable to pregnancy, childbirth, lactation etc.which would have made learning the craft of fathering compelling.

Globally, the lost art of fathering is being rediscovered. Society is discovering that great children come from homes where fathers made significant input into the upbringing of their children. Such involvement in the child's life include feeding, bathing, changing diapers in the early stage of life of the child, carrying the baby, singing lullabies to the child, reading to the child, teaching the child at home etc.

The presence of the father at home represents authority figure. Getting the child to obey the parents and all set down rules will sow the seed of responsible behavior early in the life of the child. A father should be the first school instructor in the life of his child, and should provide a foretaste of school life to his children. He does this as he undertakes to teach his child how to read, write and count figures.

The Amazing Power in Fatherhood was written to highlight practical areas in fathering which every father should be conversant with if they are to be effective fathers. An effective father is one who has endowed his children with all they need to be successful adults. With the range of topics covered in the book, every father would be given ideas of how to tackle fathering challenges in their children's lives.

Many fathers with little fathering knowledge take refuge in sending their children to reputable schools that will hopefully knock their children into shape. They forget that a father's role is irreplaceable and keeping the child away from home at the most impressionable period of the child's life is a deprivation many children never recover from even as adults. This book comes in handy in bridging the knowledge divide that will give every father the courage to do his job with grace.

The book will be particularly useful for men who grew up in fatherless homes and so were denied ab initio of firsthand experience of fathering that would have come from their biological fathers. Marriage counselors will find the book helpful in helping fathers get the right bearing when it comes to playing their role.

Francis Edo Olotu

FOREWORD

Good fathers are as priceless as the children they lead and invest in. We need effective parents especially fathers, and this book is an invaluable tool that will help meet this need. I bless God that the author, Dr Francis Edo Olotu has written it to touch all of us with his rich insight, borne out of his experiences as a family man, his extensive research in to similar works and materials, his successful career as a general medical practitioner as well as his deep knowledge of and walk with God.

Having known the author for over twenty-five years; Francis, his dear wife Bukunola [herself, a successful professional counselor, educationist, and conference speaker] and myself are the very best of friends and ministry partners. With their four lovely children[ages 12 to 23], they have formed part of my extended family and I have been privileged to spend countless hours of fellowship and interaction with this uncommon family at home, at work and at play. The children- Ufuoma, Odiri, Ejiro and Kevwe are living testimonies of what their father, the author, has enumerated in this book. Having observed first hand their well rounded upbringing, I am convinced that each of them is destined for a happy, purposeful, productive and fulfilled life. They will glorify God, bless the society and pass on their parents' good legacies to the generation following.

For this reason, I consider Dr. Olotu to be eminently qualified to write on the principles of fatherhood enunciated in this book. The author has provided a fresh look at time-tested principles for parents especially fathers, to measure their effectiveness in our modern society. Nowadays, relatively few people know or have experienced true fatherhood. Such fortunate few may have been raised, especially in their formative years by parents or guardians who provided shelter, love, care, discipline, education, vision, etc, as well as spiritual and moral values. Such individuals will find this book a refreshing reinforcement and reaffirmation of what they already know. It behoves them to with greater zeal inculcate these values to the next generation, who in turn will show others the way. The majority of people, however, have never experienced wholesome parenting and therefore, do not know how to raise or guide their own children. Many of them have even had negative examples and poor role models in their own parents; such people now need to learn positive parenting skills, especially the father.

Whatever category you fall in to, I highly recommend to you this book. While life still lasts, it is never too late to unlearn the negatives and imbibe the positives, if there is sufficient determination and commitment. With such a resource as this book and through the grace of God, you can develop in to a happy and fulfilled parent. So read on, dear reader and be blessed.

Rev John Okposio Marshal
NewBreed International, Calabar.

CHAPTER 1 THERE IS POWER IN FATHERHOOD

Every significant action of a father affects his children positively or negatively. A father's actions of today are his legacy for posterity.....Francis Edo Olotu

One of the easily visible evidence of power in fatherhood is seen in children who take after the vocation of their fathers. Many children do this without any coercion from their father. This may be attributed to the power of what they see about the profession everyday in their fathers. Some children would not take to the profession of their dad because of what they had seen at close range of the profession.

While children taking to the profession of their fathers can be described as a passive influence, there are instances when Fathers have determined the choice of the profession of their children in the very early stages of their children's lives without any consideration of the child's abilities or interests. Some opinions might consider this an abuse of the child's rights while others feel once the father has the best interest of the child at heart, he cannot be faulted.

The sporting profession has ample examples of fathers who determined the course of life of their children very early in life. In many cases, the fathers taught their children games that they were not expert in. Earl Woods, played catcher for Kansas State, the first black to play baseball in the Big Eight Conferences. He introduced Tiger to golf by swinging a club as his son watched in a high chair. He was to train Tiger in golf and watch his son evolve into the dominant player of his time. He became the youngest player to win the career Grand Slam- and one of the most celebrated and decorated sportsman of his time. He has gone down in history as the first sportsman to hit the billion dollar mark from sports earning.

Richard Williams taught his daughters Serena and Venus Williams lawn tennis very early in life and made them world champions. He had been their coach and manager from the very beginning even though all his life he never played lawn tennis. He had a fervent belief in his ability to turn his children into champions.

Mike Agassi was determined to turn at least one of his four children into a world-class player. He hung tennis balls over Andres crib, gave him full-sized racket at age 2 and while growing up made him hit 3,000 balls every day, seven days a week. He turned pro at 16 and won eight Grand slam singles titles in his career.

Mathematician Philip Emeagwali came up with a formula that let computers make 3.1billion calculations per second. He honed his skills in mathematics in a refugee camp when his father made him solve 100 mathematics problems each day in less than one hour. Dr Philip Emeagwali remains the only individual to ever win the Institute of Electrical and

Electronic Engineers Gordon Bell Prize.

The nature of the power

It is God- given; it is an extension of the paternity of God. Fatherhood or paternity is sharing in the creative power and fatherhood of God. Fathers are called to influence their children's moral and spiritual lives. Children are the supreme gift of marriage that contribute greatly to the good of society and parents themselves.

This power is released when a father creates a picture of what his child is capable of becoming in the nearest future in the mind of the child. He empowers his child with the requisite training and learning necessary to attain his/her goals. He makes himself available to guide his/her children through the various steps on the path to success and serves as a major motivator of his children in their pursuit.

God dealt with Abraham in a similar way. In Gen 13:14-16 God asked him to lift up his eyes and look: "And the Lord said to Abraham after Lot had separated from him: "Lift your eyes now and look from the place where you are- northward, southward, eastward and westward; 15 for all the land which you see I give to you and your descendants forever. 16 And I will make your descendants as the dust of the earth, then your descendants also could be numbered.17 Arise, walk in the land through its length and its width, for I give it to you". (NKJV)

God confirmed his promises to Abraham in Gen 22:15-18

Your utterances are potent

What you say to your children is very important. The way God spoke and it came to be in Genesis chapter one, so also what we say to our children has a way of coming to pass.

Proverbs 18:21 Death and Life are in the Power of the tongue, and those who love it will eat its fruit (NKJV)

A father's perception of his children determines what he says to them. If he thinks they are precious and are his ambassadors to the outside world, he would have choice, life- transforming words for them. Even when provoked, his response will be tempered by his love for his children. A good father believes he is appointed to be a blessing to his children.

A father can make the difference

July 2002 edition of the Readers Digest had a picture of the United States Secretary of State, Condoleezza Rice, age 9 taken in front of the White House gate in Washington DC. Notwithstanding being born in Birmingham

Alabama, the heart of racial segregation in 1954, her parents told her she could be the President of the United States if she so desired. This was at a time she could not enter Wal-Mart to get a burger because of her colour. Her father remembered her saying at the time the picture was taken that she would want to be in the White house one day. It became a self-fulfilling prophecy.

My own Father Daniel Obukohwo Olotu, expressed an uncommon faith in God when he declared early in 1973 that I would gain admission to study Medicine that very year. I saw his wish as a tall dream because my family finances were modest at that time and the competition for university admission was very stiff. His wish came to pass when my performance at my School Leaving Certificate Examination earned me a scholarship to study Medicine at the University of Lagos in 1973. As a teenager of 17, I was a total stranger to the powers inherent in the words of a father. I have been exercising this same power over my children with unbelievable positive results.

In 2007, my daughter Kevwe age 10, was discouraged about her persistently low scores in Mathematics, to the extent that she believed she would never gain mastery of the subject. I reassured her of her ability to master it if she adopts a positive mindset. I asked her to declare with her lips on a regular basis, "I love mathematics, I am a mathematician, God has given me the divine ability to master this subject". With ample exercises and good supervision in mathematics, her confidence grew. Today, she scores As in her mathematics tests and the mathematics teacher is her favourite teacher.

Your power is transgenerational

Your influence over your children will be transmitted over many generations for good or for evil. Your actions as a father are never neutral in their effects; they are either building up your children or creating problems in their lives. Such is the nature of the power in you.

About 40 years ago, Yale University conducted a landmark study to find out the effect of a person's lifestyle on his descendants. Two men with diametrically opposed beliefs and lifestyles were used for the study. Max Jukes who lived in New York, an atheist who believed in free sex and the abolition of all laws was one of the candidates studied. He Fathered 13 children whom he did not give Christian training. He had 1,026 descendants. Three hundred of his descendants went to prison for an average of thirteen years; 190 were prostitutes, 509 were admitted alcoholics and drug addicts.

His family at the last count had cost the State $420,000.

Jonathan Edwards was the second man studied. A disciplinarian and minister of the gospel, he was a contemporary of Max Jukes. He too fathered 13 children whom he gave Christian training. He had 929 descendants and of these 430 were Ministers of the gospel like him; 86 became University Professors, 13 became University Presidents; 75 authored books, 7 were elected into the United States Congress and 3 were State Governors. One descendant was a Vice-President of the U.S. The life of this preacher influenced generations after him.1

Fatherlessness has swelled the economic drug trade, prostitution trade, gambling industry, pornography industry, abortion, tobacco and alcohol industries. The power in fatherhood when deployed will reduce violence in schools, rebellion in homes, child suicide, lust, greed and wickedness in corporate boardroom, feminism and homosexuality. There is a subtle war to destroy the values, authority and dignity of fathers through television, news media, radio, internet and magazines. God has given man authority and dominion to preserve sanity on earth. This power should be expressed by biological fathers, adoptive fathers, step fathers, surrogate fathers, and spiritual fathers.

Summary

•The power to unlock the greatness in every child resides in his or her father.

•There are creative as well as destructive powers in your utterances to your children. Use creative utterances to motivate your child to great heights in life.

•Your power in the lives of your children will be transmitted over several generations; do not squander this valuable resource rather deploy it constructively.

Points to ponder

•As a father, in what ways have you impacted your children?

•What will your children remember you for?

• Can you replicate what Earl Woods did in the life of Tiger Woods in any aspect of your children's lives?

•Time is of the essence, you must strike while the iron is hot. Read books, listen to CDs or tapes, attend seminars on fathering, join discussion groups on the internet all in a bid to improve your fathering skills.

Further reading

1 http://self-discipline.8m.com/generational_discipline.htm

Back to top

CHAPTER 2 WHAT IS FATHERING?

A man's worth is measured by how he parents his children. What he gives them, what he keeps away from them, the lessons he teaches and the lessons he allows them to learn on their own- Lisa Rogers

Fathering is making your shoulders available for your children to stand upon so as to have a head start in life. It is shining a light on the path of life for your children to tread upon; it can be considered as life's fullest expression of masculinity in a male.

Fatherly love

This is that deep and tender feeling towards your children that makes you willing to make all necessary sacrifice in caring for them. It is measured by what you are willing to do to groom your children properly. A 1996 Gallup Poll by the National Center for Fathering found that 90.3 percent of Americans agree that "Fathers can make a unique contribution to their children's lives"1.

Your child needs you

The standard depiction of fathers in most cultures is that they exist to cater for the material needs of their children. Little is expected from them when it comes to nurturing their children. This view became entrenched after the industrial revolution when work took fathers away from home to factories. Hitherto, their presence at home meant involvement in their children's lives from infancy to adulthood. Over the years the belief in fatherhood as a valuable institution has waned, therefore society must reinvent a cultural script for fathers to assist them in their roles. There are many homes without fathers; there are also homes with fathers who are totally oblivious of their fatherly roles in their homes. Some people even believe the concept of fatherhood is superfluous.

What your child needs you for

Your child would need you in the following domains of his/her life:
Material Needs

Your children will need adequate nutrients, shelter, clothing and healthcare to promote physical and psychological development. The brain of a child grows most rapidly in the first four years of life; deprivation of food in this phase of life could affect cognitive development in the child. A study in1996, found young children living with unmarried mothers to be five times as likely to be extremely poor when compared to children in two parent homes.2

An earlier study in 1993 had found that almost 75% of American children living in single- parent families will experience poverty before they turn 11 years old as against only 20% of children in two-parent families.3

Emotional Competence

Emotional competence is the ability to manage one's emotion in a healthy and productive manner. Several studies attest to the fact that your children need you to provide support in helping them cope with basic anxieties, fears and feelings of emotional insecurity. A study assessing the level of adaptation of one-year olds found that, when left with a stranger, children whose fathers were highly involved were less likely to cry, worry, or disrupt play than other one- year olds whose fathers were less involved.4 In a 26 year longitudinal study on 379 individuals, researchers found that the single most important childhood factor in developing empathy is paternal involvement. Fathers who spent time alone with their children performing routine childcare at least two times a week, raised children who were most compassionate adults.5

Behaviour Regulation

Behavior regulation entails modeling responsible behavior to a child so that he/she grows up to imbibe and exhibit socially acceptable behavioral pattern. It is one of the prime responsibilities of a father. Many societal ills perpetrated by children have been traced to fatherlessness in many homes. A study in the State of Washington using state wide data found an increased likelihood that children born out-of- wedlock would become juvenile offenders. Compared to their peers born to married parents, a child born out-of- wedlock was:

o1.7times more likely to become an offender and 2.1times more likely to become a chronic offender if male.

o1.8times more likely to become an offender and 2.8times more likely to become a chronic offender if female.

o10 times more likely to become a chronic juvenile offender if male and born to an unmarried teen mother.6

Adolescent females between the ages of 15 and 19 years reared in homes without fathers are significantly more likely to engage in premarital sex than adolescent females reared in homes with both a mother and a father.7

Cognitive Functions

Your presence at home enhances your child's capacity to think, solve problems, set goals for him/herself and work with focused attention. Your child's memory and judgment would develop as he/she watches you take decisions in the home. Your child's ability to develop receptive and expressive skills will increase as he interacts with you in the formative phases of life.

Educational Attainment

A father's presence promotes the kind of academic learning in a child that leads to educational excellence. The spirit of competition is innate in a man and he unwittingly makes great demands on the child in academic issues. In studies involving over 25,000 children using nationally representative data sets, children who lived with only one parent had lower grade point averages, lower college aspirations, poor attendance records, and higher drop out rates than students who lived with both parents.8

Building of Social Capacity

Your child needs you to increase his/her capacity to build healthy relationships across persons of different cultures. A child's daily experience with parents affects his/her self-image and relationship with others.

Positive Father-Child relationship enhances self-acceptance, self-reliance, self-confidence and identity formation which are needed for forming good self-image and stable relationship with others. A study on attachment relationships by Cassidy et al showed that the quality of parent's care-giving behaviour initiates a process linked to the quality of peer relationships throughout childhood and early adolescence. Positive behaviour is associated with being better liked by peers. Your child needs you to help him/her choose social networks and associations that would build his interpersonal skills.

Development of Moral and Ethical Values

A father through interaction with his children can increase their capacity to understand the importance of integrity, respect for self and others, obedience to law and constituted authority. A child needs the father's input in the formation of good character. In a study using a national probability sample of 1,636 young men and women, it was found that older boys and girls from female headed households are more likely to commit criminal acts than their peers who lived with two parents.9

Spiritual Development

God expects the earliest knowledge children have of him to come from their fathers. God had this to say of Abraham in Genesis 18:19 "For I have known him, in order that he may command his children and his household after him, that they keep the way of the Lord, to do righteousness and justice, that the Lord may bring to Abraham what He has spoken to him".

Deuteronomy 6:6-7 expects the same of Fathers "And these words which I command you today shall be in your hearts. You shall teach them diligently to your children, and shall talk of them when you sit in your house, when you walk by the way, when you lie down, and when you rise up".

Summary

•Your fathering commitment is measured by what you are willing to do to groom your children properly.

•Your child needs you for his or her material needs, emotional competence, cognitive functions, educational attainment, social skills acquisition as well as moral and spiritual values development.

Points to ponder

•In what ways am I presently involved in the lives of my children?

• Do I have a developmental agenda for them?

Further reading

1   Gallup Poll, 1996. National Center For Fathering. "Father Figures". Today's Father 4.1 (1996):8.

2 One in four: Americas Youngest Poor. National Center for children in poverty. 1996

3 National Commission on Children. Just the Facts: Summary of Recent Information on   America's Children and their Families. Washington, DC, 1993

4 Kotelchuk, M. The Infants Relationship to His Father: Experimental Evidence.The Role pf the Father in Child Development. By Michael Lamb.2nd ed. New York: Wiley,1981.

5 Koestner, Richard, Carol Franz, and Joel Weinberger. The Family Origins of Empathic Concern: A Twenty- Six Longitudinal study. Journal of personality and Social Psychology 58 (1990): 709-717.

6 Conseur, Amy et all. Maternal and Perinatal Risk Factors for Later Delinquency.

7 Billy, John O.G..,Karin L Brewster and William R.Grady. Contextual Effects on the Sexual Behaviour of Adolescent Women. Journal of Marriage and Family 56(1994): #81-404.

8 McLanahan, Sara and Gary sandefur. Growing up with a single Parent: What Hurts, What Helps. Cambridge: Harvard University Press,1994

9 Heimer, Karen. Gender Interaction and Delinquency: Testing a Theory of Differential Social Control. Social Psychology Quarterly 59 (1996):39-61.

Back to top

CHAPTER 3 DIFFERENT STROKES OF FATHERING

I cannot think of any need in childhood as strong as the need for a father's protection- Sigmund Freud

There are different types of Dads with each category reflecting a composite of their genetic endowment and environmental influence in their actions. The most important influence in predicting a man's fathering skills is what he got from his own father while growing up. What a man gets from his father is an amalgam of what his father taught him, what he did with his father and what he observed his father do. At no time is a father's actions devoid of consequences, in fact his actions at any time constitute his legacy for posterity. A father lives on in his children for good or for evil.

A man's level of education affects his fathering skills because education enables him to read about fathering, attend seminars on fatherhood, observe some families with successful children and draw inferences from what he sees. It is an educated mind that seeks to know why some men succeed at raising their children while others are a dismal failure in this task; he finally resolves on what new ideas to incorporate into fathering his children.

The aphorism Nemo dat non quod habet: You cannot give what you do not have is particularly true with fathering. Fatherless children grow to become fatherless adults who in turn sire fatherless children. The expression fatherlessness describes children who grew up in one-parent home as well those who had fathers that were not involved physically and emotionally in their upbringing.

Different types of fathers. We shall consider 4 types of dads in this section.

Authoritative/Empowering father

This type of father is acutely aware of the type of fathering he got while growing up. He therefore strives to give his children what he never had as a child but which he believes will help his children become responsible adults. This type of father is usually educated, having a good job, more trusting and often comes from a background where responsible fatherhood had been modeled for him

He exhibits paternal tenderness in a companionate marriage setting. He recognizes that his wife shares in his authority and her role is irreplaceable, he shows this in his love for his wife. He actively shares parental responsibilities with his wife. Together with his wife, he regulates the behavior of their children and applies consistent, fair and proportionate disciplinary measures for inappropriate behavior. He usually provides the finances for his children's needs and education.

He admits that the role of a father goes beyond that of providing for the material needs of his children to participating in nurturing his children to adulthood. He is willing to go beyond gender stereotype which restricts fathers to certain roles in the home. He demonstrates love for children, makes quality time available to be with his children and communicates with his children on the issues of life. He affirms his children, motivates them to success in life, counsels them and emphasizes good character formation. He shows interest in their education, and he is part of his children's support system. He blesses his children, prays with and for them. He believes in the rule of law and teaches his children to be law abiding. He models responsible behavior to his children and brings them up in a way that will help them to be successful

Authoritarian/Disciplinarian father

This type of father believes in the old concept of fatherhood. Typically, he is aloof, distant and authoritarian. His words are laws that leave no room for appeal or negotiation. He does not respect his children's point of view in any issue. He harbors free-floating hostilities and may be described as a time bomb waiting to explode at the slightest provocation. Very often such fathers try to beat out of their children what they perceive is wrong in their lives He is often not very educated and so may not avail himself of opportunities to acquire better fathering skills. He may be engaged in a low paying job. He does not believe in sharing parental responsibilities with his children's mother and may even be physically abusive to her. No doubt some of these fathers had abusive backgrounds. Emotions are rarely expressed in this concept of fatherhood. They tended to follow the pattern they experienced from their own fathers.

Some of the bloodiest chapters in 20th century history were written by persons who came from abusive homes. They were primed for violence early in childhood and grew to become liabilities to society because of what they suffered as children. Adolf Hitler was so often beaten by his father especially after a spell of drinking that on one occasion his father thought he had killed him. Joseph Stalin, years after being beaten by his often drunken father developed a strange fascination with the idea of pain and showed no compassion or love for animals or other humans. Saddam Hussein also had an abusive childhood.

Passive fathers

This type of father lives in the same house with his children but is not involved emotionally or physically in their lives.

He leaves parental responsibilities for the children's mother and when anything goes wrong with the children, he is quick to point accusing fingers at the wife for failing in her parental duties. One passive father wondering how his son became rebellious had this to say, "I don't know what Victoria could have done wrong raising Anselm. I know it wasn't anything I did, since I put in all my resources trying to make more money for the family and left him for her. I barely had time for the boy, so, there is no way I would have influenced him negatively".

Such men often come from a background where their father was passive. He does not make any input in building the children's self-esteem, self-worth or self-confidence. He may provide financial support for his children.

A story was told of a man whose routine was going to work early in the morning while the children were still in bed and returning late in the evening after they had gone to sleep. One day, he had to stay at home because of ill health. In the morning his perplexed children asked their mother who the stranger was that was sleeping on the bed; the mother told them he was their dad. They refused to accept what she told them. Barely an hour later, a man appeared who regularly ate at the woman's canteen and whom the children surrogately called daddy. The children chorused daddy and ran to his warm embrace. Needless to say, their father was embarrassed and decided to quit his job to reclaim his children.

Henry B.Biller, in a 1994 unpublished paper titled " The Father Factor and the Two-Parent Advantage; Reducing the Paternal deficit"- said: in 2-parent households, fewer than 25% of young boys and girls experience an average of at least one hour a day of relatively individualized contact with their fathers. The average daily amount of one- to- one father/child contact reported in US is less than 30minutes.

Absent/disengaged fathers

These are fathers who do not live in the same house with their children. Fatherlessness in the literal and metaphorical sense always has negative consequences for society. Paternal disinvestment occurs in divorce when the wife has custody of the children and the man abdicates his fathering responsibilities to his children, when children are borne out of wedlock and raised in single parent homes and when fathers become economic migrants and live apart from the family to provide for the family. The vacuum created by the absence of a father is not easily filled by either maternal investment or an effective web of social services. Over 50% of children in North America will grow up at some point in a single parent home. 1/3 of live births are to unmarried women. Over 1 million men with children under 18 are in prison. Thousands of children loose their fathers to untimely death from accident and illnesses. Alcohol, drugs and imprisonment deprive children of fathers input into their lives. Fatherless children are 2-5 times more likely to drop out of school. 75% of persons in drug abuse treatment centers come from fatherless homes. 90% of homeless and runaway teens come from fatherless homes. 71% of teen pregnancies are children of single parents. 75% of all teen suicides are to children of single parents. Children of single parents are 2-3 times more likely o have emotional and behavioral problems. 85% of all youths in prisons grew up in fatherless home.

According to the 1994 census Bureau data released in 1996, 39% of children under 18 (27,341,000 children) live apart from their biological fathers. The National Commission on Children's national survey of children and parents (1991) found close to half of all children in disrupted families hadn't seen their fathers in the past year. Nearly 1 in 5 children in female-headed families hadn't seen their fathers in 5 years. Frank Furstenberg (Divided Families, 1991) said more than one- half of all children who don't live with their father have never been in their father's home.

As of June 1994, there were an estimated 778,761 dads in prison with children under 18, and another 105,500 dads whose only children were over 18 (Bureau of Justice Statistics).

Other types of fathers

Dead beat dad- This dad jettisons his gender-based duty of providing for his children, he casts the role of a father in a superfluous light. Such a father has rejected responsibility for his children.

Visiting father- This is a father who visits and keeps contact with his children after divorce. He pays child support without creating scenes. The emotional bond between such fathers and their children is very weak because of his continual absence in the life of his children. Father-child daily communication that is a critical aspect of fathering is missing.

Summary

•The choice of the type of father a man wants to be is entirely his. He could be an authoritative/empowering father, an authoritative/disciplinarian father, passive father, or an absent/disengaged father.

•At the other of the spectrum are dead beat and visiting fathers.

•You may fall into one of these categories by choice or by default.

Points to ponder

•What kind of a father are you?

•It is never too late to change your fathering style so that one day, your children would celebrate you for the difference you made in their lives.

Further reading

Hawkins, A. & Dollahite, D. (1997). Generative Fathering: Beyond deficit perspectives. Thousand Oaks, CA:Sage

Levine, J.A. & Pitt, E. W. (1995). New Expectations: Community Strategies for Responsible Fatherhood. New York: Work & Families Institute.

Back to top

CHAPTER 4 THE GOOD NEWS OF FATHERHOOD AWAKENING

One father is more than a hundred schoolmasters-George Herbert

Globally, there is an awakening of interest in the hearts of men on the subject of fatherhood. The reasons for this may not be far-fetched. Growing recognition of the problems caused by fathers' absence is one of the main reasons. Closely related to this is the fact that many men are getting more knowledgeable about the importance of their roles in their children's lives. Hitherto the mindset of many fathers had been that, bringing home the paycheck was all that was needed for them to fulfill their fathering role. The ever increasing knowledge base on the effect of fatherlessness had caused many fathers to abandon this mindset. To the Poll question "when making important family decisions, consideration of the children should come first", an advertising agency's annual "lifestyle Survey" found that for men in 18-24 age bracket, those who said yes increased from 66% in 1986 to 81% in 1995. For men over 25years, those who answered yes increased from 60% in 1986 to 66% in 1995. Another evidence of the growing commitment of young fathers is the number of dads present at their children's births which has risen from 27% in 1974 to 90% today.

Fathers have come to realize that they are capable of giving their children what their own father did not give them while growing up. They are willing to exceed physical and verbal nurturing to be more involved in their children's lives. At DuPont Corp, a 1995 study concluded "the most striking finding is the positive impact that DuPont's work-life program has had on business results. In their study of 18,000 employees, the company found that the top 3 reasons employees rejected changes in their duties or promotions were family related. They had refused: relocation 34%, increased travel 24% and overtime or job with more pressure 21%".

The increase in the number of women taking up paid jobs to augment family income implies that fathers at sometime must assume more responsibilities at home. This has brought down the walls of stereotypes which limited fathers to certain functions in the homes and opened the door to more involvement in their children's lives. The tripling of the divorce rate in America between 1960 and 1980 with its devastating effects on parents and their children served as a case study for the rest of the world on the need to work hard at having successful marriages.

Other parts of the world also experienced an increase in divorce rate with its consequences. Remarriage and step fathering are not attractive options to many men who will rather work at their marriage to see that it succeeds.

Many corporate organizations are beginning to see the link between happy family situations and better performance at work. Some have gone as far as providing day care centers for children of their employees while others have family enrichment activities. A 1987 fortune magazine poll found 30% of fathers said they had personally turned down a job promotion or transfer because it would have reduced the time they spend with their families. In a 1991 survey, 75% of the men said they would trade rapid career advancement for the chance to leave more time open to their families. (Dallas Morning News)

Summary
•Fathers every where are discovering the powers within them and are releasing this power to lift their children to greater heights in life.

•Some fathers are deliberately turning down job promotions in order to have more time for their family.

Points to ponder

•Have you keyed into the fatherhood awakening?

•What recent measure(s) have you taken to improve your fathering skills? You can read books or attend seminars whose theme is on the family.

Further reading

Marsiglio, W. (1993). Contemporary Scholarship on Fatherhood: Culture, Identity, and Conduct. Journal of Family Issues, 14(4), 484-509

Parke, R.D. (1996). Fatherhood. Cambridge, M.A: Harvard University Press

Back to top

CHAPTER 5 HOW FATHERS INFLUENCE EARLY CHILDHOOD DEVELOPMENT

It doesn't matter who my father was, it matters who I remember he was
Anne Sexton

A child's personality has its roots in the early experiences of life. This affects the child's thinking, emotions, learning ability and behavior in life. Perception, memory and sense of judgment of a child develop most rapidly in the first 3 years of life, and this corresponds with the period of most rapid growth of the child's brain. The family environment among other factors such as ill health can affect this phase of the child's life either positively or negatively. Understandings how your child's mind works at any point in time would enable you relate better with him/ her as well as empower you to help your child develop into a well adjusted adult. Knowledge about this aspect of his/ her life will assist you in resolving some developmental challenges confronting your child.

At each stage in life, you can seek to understand your child in terms of his/ her:

•Perception- how the child views the world

•Motivation- what makes the child behave in a particular way.

•Learning- how experience teaches the child.

•Thinking- how the child solves problems.

•Emotions- how the child feels about his/ her world.

Formation of attachment(bonding)

First Year of life is when a child forms strong bonds with the mother first and later the father. Babies become attached to fathers who spend enough time with them to know what they need when they cry or display other emotions. The effects of attachment are life-long; separation at this period of life hampers the child's ability to form intimate social relationships in future. One study found primary school children who are attached to their fathers to be more empathic- they had the ability to see a situation from another person's view point and are quick to observe sadness in their friends. Such children recognized how other children felt and took steps to make them feel better; in other words, they are more affectionate.

What play does for children

Play time gives children opportunities to investigate the world around them, manipulate objects and explore physical relationships. Fathers, because of their vigorous ways of playing with their children, provide more physical and verbal stimulation during play and this helps in the development of the child's brain. It also has positive impact on the child's social, emotional and intellectual development; making such children score high on tests of thinking skills and brain development. One study found such baby boys to be more popular than their mates at school because they socialize readily with their mates.

To toddlers

Increased play activities mark this phase of life. A father's presence keeps the child from hurting him/herself by his setting appropriate limits to the extent of play. Normal physiological development at this phase involves motor development which manifests in increased physical activities and growing sensory perception. The child also develops emotionally in how he/she expresses feelings and socially in how he/she interacts with people. Development of language skills and intellectual development that relate to acquiring problem solving skills occur in this phase of life.

What do children learn from their fathers during play in this phase of life?

They learn how to solve problems and how to get along with others. Through rough and tumble play, fathers create obstacles for their children and demand respect for limits and boundaries. At the same time, they challenge their children and encourage them to explore their own strength and learn new skills.

In pre-school years

This corresponds to the 4th and 5th year of life when the child develops conscience. The child internalizes what is socially acceptable by the parents and develops a sense of guilt. A child's capacity to feel guilty later in life will be impaired if he/ she doesn't have stable relationship with the parents at this phase of life.

Development of emotional knowledge

Playing with fathers helps children identify their own emotions while acknowledging the emotional experience of others. Fathers who do this teach their children how to express their emotions responsibly and control their behaviours. Children who understand and control their emotions are easier to get along with at school. They have learnt to give and take; they have learnt they cannot have their way all the time. Children who have fathers that acknowledge their emotions and help them deal with bad emotions, score high on tests of "emotional intelligence".

What is the effect of this?

They have better relationship with other children and behave less aggressively because their fathers have helped them build strong social skills.

Father's influence at elementary school level

Children learn new skills and how to cope with challenges and failure at this phase of life. The quality of a father's involvement at this stage determines whether the child develops the confidence and competence required to meet new challenges in a positive manner. A sense of industry or a belief that he or she can accomplish a goal or master a skill is important in a child's development of a sense of self-esteem. Fathers do this by giving their children new challenges that make them learn independence and acquire more problem solving skills. By learning new skills, children take responsibility for their actions and learn not to blame others for mistakes. Influence of Fathers on Children's learning at this stage

Fathers' influence improves the child's performance at school because

•They provide better economic support which means better access to educational resources and opportunities to learn; attendance at good schools improves.

•Fathers spend good time helping them with their homework and so can identify their learning needs.

•Learning becomes a continuous experience when a father is involved. A study has found that 4 and 5 year olds scored higher in Maths tests when fathers made their children read and count. A study found children whose fathers encouraged them in sport and fitness activities were more successful in school and in their careers later in life. This is because the discipline they acquired in sports helps in every other area of life.

•Fathers help children adjust to school life when they start schooling. They prevent excessive absence and poor academic performance. Even children with Attention Deficit/Hyperactivity Disorder who have supportive fathers adjust better when their fathers are involved in their care.

•Personal Moral Development is influenced by fathers at this age by the guidance they provide. They also give moral instructions as well as emphasize good behaviour. Fathers also serve as role models for their children; they model good behaviour to them. Children who had good attention from their fathers at this period grow up to be more understanding and socially responsible adults.

Summary

•A father can seek to understand his child early in life in the different developmental domains.

•Bonding or attachment to a child occurs from spending time with the child.

•A father's influence at the elementary school level helps the child develop confidence and competence.

Points to ponder

•Is your child having any behavioural problem that needs your attention or professional help? Attend to him/her on time.

•Time spent with your children in early childhood will create a bank of unforgettable memories for your children.

Further reading

Lamb, M.E. (1997) The Role of the Father in Child Development, 3rd Edn. New York: Wiley

Back to top

CHAPTER 6 A FATHER AND HIS TEENAGER

When I was a boy of fourteen, my father was so ignorant I could hardly stand to have the old man around. But when I got to be twenty-one, I was astonished at how much he had learned in seven years. ~Mark Twain

The teenage years are the transition period from childhood to young adulthood that is characterized by rapid physical changes coupled with development of secondary sexual characteristics. Adolescence is the very early part of this phase which is dominated by physical and psychological changes brought about by puberty. This is a very important phase in the child's life because success at this usually produces a well adjusted adult. A father's presence, understanding and guidance is needed to see the child through this turbulent period.

Identity development

This involves a child knowing who he/ she is, his/her values and the direction to follow in life. There may be a temporary period of confusion and distress as the child comes to terms with a sense of identity before settling on values and goals in life. A child who scales this hurdle successfully becomes a mature adult.

How a father can help his child through this stage?

A father's availability and accessibility would help the child communicate his/her feelings while at the same time seeking the father's approval.

Feedback from the father raises the child's self- esteem. Schools and communities that provide rich and varied opportunities for self exploration aid the child at this period.

Extracurricular activities that promote high level thinking which enables the teenager take responsible roles foster identity achievement.

At the end of this phase, a significant achievement will be the child's self- description which has become more organized and consistent with personal and moral values.

Psycho-social development

There are changes in the child's mind that affect social relationships. The child wants autonomy. He/she wants to become an independent, self governing person within relationships. A child who succeeds at this phase is able to make and follow through with his/her decision, live by his/her own set of principles of right and wrong and becomes less emotionally dependent on parents. This step is necessary for the child to be a self- sufficient adult.

The craving for intimacy in this phase is a desire for caring, honest and trusting relationship. Initially, this should be at the level of same gender relationship; experience at this level will be helpful when the child is older and indulges in romantic relationship with the complimentary gender.

Friendship provides a setting in which young people can practice their social skills with those who are their equals.

Friends provide a platform for teenagers to learn how to begin, maintain and terminate relationship, practice social skills and become intimate.

Also at this phase of life, they receive conflicting messages about their sexuality in life. They display shyness, blushing and modesty and worry about their looks. They are concerned about their physical and sexual attractiveness to others.

As part of the intellectual growth which is characteristic of this phase, the teenager appreciates the link between their current abilities and their future vocation.

Intellectual development

The child's thinking skills improve and help the child think about multiple options and possibilities in any given situation. The power of logical and hypothetical thinking develops, likewise that of abstract thinking. The adolescent is able to evaluate his/her own way of thinking and feeling as well as how others perceive him/her. He/she is able to provide solutions to academic challenges facing him/her.

Experimentation with sex and drugs such as cigarettes, alcohol and marijuana is common at this phase and is quite often the result of peer pressure.

How a father can help his child in this stage of life

•Allow the child spend quality time with his/her friends so that he/ she can develop and acquire more social skills.

•Be willing to answer your child's questions about adult values and beliefs. For instance, your child may want to know the advantages and disadvantages of abstinence.

•Allow him/her to establish his/her privacy at home by locking the door to his or her room or demanding that you knock before entering his/her room.

•Be willing to tell your child your experiences as a teenager when he/she demands to know. It is part of trying to relate with you as an adult.

•Educate them about their sexuality and measures to be taken to develop a healthy sexual life. Tell them what true masculinity and feminity are all about.

•Teenage girls may find self- esteem in their relationships with mothers and guidance on how to relate to others.

•They would learn how to plan for the future by their relationship with their father

Summary

•A teenager undergoes identity, psycho-social and intellectual development during this phase of life.

•There are different ways by which good father-child relationship enables the child succeed in this phase of life.

Points to ponder

•What are the challenges confronting your child in this phase of life?

•What is the most challenging behavioural problem you helped your teenage child overcome?

Further reading

David Elkind. All Grown Up and No Places to Go

Jeamer Lerche Davis. 10 Parenting Tips for Raising Teenagers. Available at http://www.webmd.com/parenting/guide/10-parenting-tips-for-raising-teenagers

Back to top

CHAPTER 7 KNOW YOUR CHILD

It is a wise father that knows his own child-William Shakespeare

Every child is a deep reservoir of talents and skills waiting to be unveiled. Knowledge of your child deepens your understanding of the child and enables you to relate better with him/her. Since a father is well positioned to offer the child appropriate advice to advance his/her chances in life, the time taken to know one's child is a time well invested with a promise of rich dividends.

You need to develop keen listening skills to know what he/she is saying and what he/she is not saying if you want to be of help to him.

Using open ended questions in your discussions such as "what challenges did you face at school today?" instead of " Was school interesting today?" would let you know how he is coping at school. A good sense of observation would tell you a lot about his/her interests very early in life Knowledge of your child in these areas is crucial to effective fathering.

Temperament

Temperament is an aggregate of inborn traits in a child that determines how a child perceives the world and relates to it. It is his/her basic inherited style of life; it can be likened to the canvas on which the painting of his/her life was made. In contrast, personality is the actual painting on the canvas; it is the effect of the environment on your temperament. Environmental influence includes parental influence, home environment, education, socialization, birth order, siblings etc, etc.

Knowing your child's temperament is advantageous in the following ways:

•It gives you a clue on how to raise your child.

•It tells you how the child sees him/herself and others.

•It prevents you from blaming yourself or the child for issues that are normal for the child's temperament e.g. a very gregarious child or moody child can be as a result of the temperament.

•It prevents you from rushing to the doctor for issues that are simply a child's expression of his/her temperament.

•It enables you to anticipate issues that might present difficulties to the child.

•You will feel more effective as a father as you fully understand and appreciate your child's personality.

•It makes you understand the strengths and weaknesses of your child.

•You can more effectively work in line with your child's temperament instead of working in opposition to it. When the child needs adaptation to the environment, he/she will find in you a knowledgeable partner.

•Your knowledge of your child's temperament will help you guide him/her in the choice of vocation.

Personality types

Psychologists since ancient times have grouped people into 4 basic personality types: Sanguine, Phlegmatic, Choleric and Melancholic.

There are 16 subtypes which are a combination of the 4 major personality types e.g. phlegmatic/melancholic.

The first two types are extroverts in their disposition while the later two are introverts. Most persons are a mix of these four personality types.

Sanguine A child can be considered sanguine if he/she is lively, outgoing, likes to have people around him and speaks persuasively. He makes friend easily and with him/her there can be no dull moment. He/she will make a good salesperson. His/her weakness or liability is lack of discipline and modesty with a tendency to exaggerating situations. They can exhibit poor self control in speaking, eating and alcohol intake. They can also be "morally flexible" and quick to explain away their moral failings.

Choleric This child is forceful, decisive, strong-willed, independent and strongly opinionated. He/she is a beehive of activities and has strong leadership skills. He/she can fly into a rage at the slightest provocation and could be ruthless in his/her dealings. His/her shortcomings are poorly developed emotions that bother on being affectionless and a tendency to ride roughshod over people.

Melancholy This child is prone to moodiness, is introverted, very self-critical, analytical with perfectionist tendencies. He/she does not make friends easily because he/she suspects people. They can be self-sacrificing and may be inclined to professions like medicine and nursing where they have opportunities to give care. Their weak point is their tendency to be unforgiving, and to keep account of wrongs done against them. They can also suffer from persecution complex where they think everybody is against them.

Phlegmatic This child is easy going, mild tempered reserved, humorous, gets along with people but can be timid. He/she can be very dependable; will rarely volunteer to do any task though when appointed to lead, they make good leaders. A lot of teachers and administrators are of this temperament. Their weakness is in their stubbornness, lack of drive or initiative and wanting "peace at all cost". Rather than confronting an issue, they wish it away and in this way the problem is prolonged.

Interests

Every child is unique, quite often his/her uniqueness is revealed in his/her interests. Spending time with your child, listening to him/her, watching her play or communicate with others could reveal her line of interest. The interest may be in music, painting, sports, reading, etc. Your child's interest may be age-related and so may change with time.

Strengths and weaknesses

Knowledge of his/her strengths and weaknesses will enable you counsel her especially with regards to relationships and career.

Heroes/Heroines

Knowing your child's heroes/heroines tells you a lot about what is going on in his/her mind, and asking him/her what he/she likes in these persons will let you know his/her set of values. You can address some critical issues about life based on what is good or bad in his/her hero/heroine.

Most treasured possession

This would tell you a lot about his/her set of values and give you an opportunity to talk about critical life issues.

Favorite food

Know it so that you can give him/her a treat when you think he/she deserves one

Favorite color

Knowledge of this would enable you buy presents and dresses that he/she would appreciate.

Fears/Stresses

You can deal with this if they are rational and reassure your child if they are irrational.

Aspirations

When you know this, you are able to align with your child to achieve his/her goals.

Use of spare time

What he/she does with his/her spare time reveals the line of interest and presents an opportunity for useful discussion on life and vocation.

Favorite uncle/aunt

This would give you an insight into what he/she likes in people as well as his/her type of person.

Happiest moments

You can work to create more of this in his/her life.

Saddest moments

You can work to avoid such incidents.

What he/she likes or dislikes in you

This provides a valuable feedback in your relationship that would bring about changes in your interactions and promote cordiality.

His/her most priced accomplishment last year

This is a window into what he/she values and can provide opportunity for meaningful discussion.

Summary

•Knowledge of your child deepens your understanding of him/her and promotes good father-child relationship because it reduces friction between you.

•Knowing your child's temperament and personality type helps you in raising him or her.

Points to ponder

•Can you describe the temperament of each of your children alongside their strengths and weaknesses?

•In what areas would you want to work with them to overcome their weaknesses?

Further reading

Stella Chess, Alexander Thomas. Know Your Child: An Authoritative Guide to Today's Parents

Back to top

Chapter Eight Enhancing Your Child's Learning Ability

Every child has the potential to learn far beyond his or her parent's expectation. It is your duty to encourage each child to want to learn, to enjoy learning and to be capable of studying whatever they need or wish to be in future-Toru Kumon

Learning is a very important process in the life of every child, success at learning is an important predictor of a child's socioeconomic attainment in life. Because learning embodies discipline, those who are successful at it invariably attain success in other spheres of life where discipline plays a pivotal role. There is a strong correlation between student achievement and the expectations placed on them by their parents with some exceptions though. America with its mixed culture had provided the case study from which the above conclusions were drawn. African-American and Latino parents tended to be satisfied with any grade above a D and their children return mostly Cs. White parents are satisfied with anything above a C and their children earn mostly Bs; while Asian parents demand the lowest grade of an A- and their children bring mostly As. The conclusion is that on the average students deliver mostly what their parents ask for. Studies have debunked the myth that high academic achievers are stressed and unhappy kids when it revealed that Asian students who do well at school report the lowest rates of depression, headaches, drug and alcohol use while at the same time enjoying a robust circle of friends.

Helping your child to learn

Every child has a unique learning style which is partly inherited and partly influenced by the environment. Your duty as a father is to find out how your child learns. A lot of light was shed on how children process and learn information through the pioneering work of Dr Howard Gardner, a Professor of Education at Harvard University. His theory of Multiple Intelligences describes 9 ways by which children express themselves. They are:

•Linguistic Intelligence Children with this ability are good listeners, fluent in speech, have extensive vocabulary, good communicators, have a flair for learning different languages and often excel in English language and social studies in comparison to mathematics and science. Encourage such a child to read novels and discuss them. A career in writing, law or teaching may suit such a child.

•Logical-Mathematical Intelligence Children with this ability love figures, mathematics as a subject and like to know how things work. Such a child can be engrossed with the computer and love asking questions on a variety of subjects. A career in science, engineering, medicine or accountancy will be exciting to such a child.

•Spatial Intelligence A child with this ability will love charts, maps and drawing. Engaging such a child with painting and drawing will be exciting while a career in fine arts, architecture or interior decoration will be fulfilling

•Body-Kinesthetic Intelligence Such children enjoy physical activities and can excel in more than one sport. Encourage such a child to indulge in extracurricular activities that will hone his skills. A career in sports and calisthenics will be fulfilling to such a child.

•Musical Intelligence Such a child loves music, remembers melodies and knows when music is off-key. Encourage the child to learn to play different musical equipments while a career in music, song writing, singing and composition will be fulfilling.

•Interpersonal Intelligence A child with this skill socializes well and can be a natural leader because he has his way with people. Participating in collaborative activities will hone this skill while a career in counseling, teaching,marketing and public relations may be satisfying.

•Intrapersonal Intelligence Such a child is very self confident and self reliant and capable of working alone on assignments. A career in research will be stimulating to such a child.

•Naturalist Intelligence Such a child is in love with nature and loves outdoor activities especially when it has to do with forests, animals and zoo. A career in biology, botany, zoology and other related fields will be appealing to such a child.

•Existential Intelligence Such a child portrays a philosophical awareness that is above his/her years in the type of questions he/she asks. Such a child thinks a lot and may opt for a career in philosophy or priesthood.

The bottom line about childhood learning is that your child may not know his/her learning style until he/she is exposed to different stimuli.

Learning disability

Some children experience difficulties with learning. It's been found that such difficulties are associated with processing certain type of information. While learning disability has no known cure for now, adapting to it and learning strategies to surmount the problem will help the child accomplish his/her goals and dreams in life. It is reassuring to know that the condition does not affect a person's intelligence. The list of persons who had this challenge and surmounted it to make their mark in life includes Alexander Graham Bell, Thomas Edison, Beethoven, Albert Einstein, George Washington, John F. Kennedy, Bill Cosby, Benjamin Franklin and Walt Disney. Your child can be among the greats if you give him/her the needed assistance and be a strong part of his/her support system.

The difference a father's involvement makes in the child's school

There are compelling facts from the US National Center for Education Statistics that show that a father's involvement in the child's school whether he is resident or non-resident has salutary effects on the child's performance. The level of participation ranges from attendance at general meetings, regularly scheduled parent-teacher conferences, class or school events to volunteering for a service at your child's school.

It is beneficial to the child in the following ways:

•Appraisal of the School Participation in your child's school makes you more familiar with the school and how it runs. This insider knowledge enables you to intervene early should there be a problem in your child's academics and behaviour. Familiarity with your children's teachers would lead to a better parent-teacher relationship and a more personal attention for your children.

•Better Academic Performance Children enjoy school more and are more likely to have excellent grades when their fathers are involved. Father involvement in the child's school also reduces the chances of a child repeating a class or grade particularly at elementary school level. It also reduces the chances of a child being suspended or expelled from school on account of bad behaviour because the father is able to regulate his/her behavior before it gets out of hand.

•School is Important Your involvement in your child's school convinces your child that school is important and enables you to convey to your children your educational expectations. It is also a reflection of your level of commitment to your child.

•Participation in other activities It's been found that fathers who participate in the school activities of their children also share in other activities of their children. This strengthens the father-child bond

•Building social capital Fathers who participate in school activities are more likely to belong to church, union and professional associations which invariably have family activities that provide children opportunities to build their social networks.

•Involvement in extracurricular activities Children are more likely to participate in extracurricular activities when their fathers are involved in their schools. Sports, music and other activities that bring in parents as spectators, coaches or advisors can be appealing to children.

•Parental coalition When a father is involved in the children's school, the mother quite often gets more involved in her children's school and together they become partners that further their children's educational fortunes.

•Better school climate Parents' input into their children's school often results in better school climate because they are able to make informed input into the running of the school. Such inputs should result in greater classroom/school discipline and greater respect between teachers and pupils which will lead to improvement in the school climate.

Summary

•It is within the power of every father to enhance his child's learning ability.

•It is the duty of a father to find out how his child learns to enable him give him/her the needed assistance.

•A child with learning disability can be assisted in surmounting his/her disability.

•A father's involvement in his child's school improves the child's school performance.

Points to ponder

•In what ways have you encouraged your children to excel in their learning efforts?

•Always remember that you can be the most important influence in your child's education.

Further reading

Cheri Fuller: Opening Your Child's Nine Learning Windows
Edward M. Hallowell, MD{2000} Practical Tips to Help Your Child to
Learn Better and to Value Education. Available at
http://www.Idonline.org/article/Practical_Tips_to_Help_Your_Child_to_Lear

Back to top

CHAPTER 9 HOW MARRIAGE IMPACTS FATHERING

Father taught us that opportunity and responsibility go hand in hand. I think we all act on that principle; on the basic human impulse that makes a man want to make the best of what's in him and what's been given him. ~Laurence Rockefeller

Children do not blossom in a vacuum; they need an enabling environment to thrive. This environment comprises significant persons in the child's life such as parents, siblings, grand parents, teachers, school mates, the home, school, neighborhood and the society at large. Genetic endowment and environmental influence affect the growth and development of children.

How a happy marriage impacts fathering

A happy marriage is one in which the husband, wife and children are living in harmony. An atmosphere of love is critical to childhood development. Parental harmony provides a strong sense of security to children. In an ideal home environment, children are taught morals in an age-appropriate and culture-compliant manner. They are taught to distinguish between good and evil and to shun evil at all times. Anecdotes, contemporary events and wise sayings are used to drive home valuable points.

Other ways by which a happy marriage promotes fathering are as follows:

Guarantees father presence in the home A peaceful home provides the enabling environment for the father to spend quality time at home with the children. Men tend to keep away from home when there is strife and so they loose the opportunity to nurture their children at the critical phases of their development. For fathers to be effective, they need the support, encouragement and skills- building environment which a happy marriage provides. When a marriage is not happy, a father may be physically present but psychologically absent, and therefore makes little input in the grooming of his children.

An except from one essay in the Essay contest organized by US National Center For Fathering reads:

"I don't know what it is to have a father. I see people that have one and wish I had mine. I have always wanted to feel the love of a father. Sometimes my days are bad and I cry because I need someone there to talk to, to share my troubles, my fears and most of all my dreams. I have been through a lot of bad moments and if he would have been there none of these would have happened because he would have been there to protect me. I feel empty inside." (11th grader whose father abandoned her and her mom when she was 2).

Partnership A husband who loves and respects the wife and who commands the children to do same, would find in the wife a partner in nurturing his children to responsible adulthood. Such a couple would provide a united front to the children on matters of discipline, morals and academic pursuit. Such children would find in their parents models for responsible parenthood.

Policy implementation It is a happy wife that implements family policies when the husband is away to work. When a mother monitors her children in line with the husband's wishes or directives, the evidence of good fathering would be there for all to see.

Inputs A happy wife makes suggestions to the husband based on what she perceives are the children's need. In this way she helps her husband in providing total care for the growing children.

Financial support It is a happy working wife that augments the family budget to provide for some of the needs of the children. In a happy marriage, the husband strives to meet his financial obligation to the family.

Feedback A happy wife gives feedback to her husband on his fathering efforts. She identifies what more needs to be done by the father in the life of his children.

Promotes openness among the children Happiness between husband and wife is infectious; it has a way of spreading to the rest of the family. In such an environment, children communicate their feelings and needs to their parents more readily than they would do in a strife-torn home. A home where physical affection such as hugs and kisses are expressed, and where compliments are liberally paid produces well adjusted, affectionate children with strong self-esteem.

Dr Lee Salk in his book "My Father, My Son" relayed a scene in his interview with Mark Chapman, the convicted slayer of Beatle John Lennon, Chapman declared at one point in the interview "I don't think I ever hugged my father. He never told me he loved me……….. I needed emotional love and support. I never got that" Chapman further said if he ever had a son "I would hug my son and kiss him……….and just let him know……he could trust me and come to me …. And would tell him that I loved him"

There is no alternative to marriage as a foundation for happy family

Marriage as an institution is under attack from many fronts, however compelling data from many researches underscore its relevance today more than any other time in history. One revealing study found that only 36% of children born to cohabiting couples live with both parents during their entire childhood compared to 70% of children born within a marriage. This shows that the level of commitment in cohabiting relationship is lower than what it is in marriage. To promote support for marriage among fathers the following measures are appropriate:

Prevention of Fatherlessness programs should be increased rather than just addressing the consequences of fatherlessness. Men need to understand that establishing their marriages on solid footing before becoming fathers and continuing to work on their marriages are powerful antidotes to this scourge of fatherlessness afflicting society.

The most effective strategy for working with fathers in a way that translates into improvement in the well being of children is to have a good marriage. Cohabitation, child support enforcement, enhanced visitation, foster homes are all poor substitutions for a strong happy marriage.

If we want to make a real difference in the lives of our children, we must seek to build happy marriages. Fatherhood programs must not be ambivalent towards the issue of better marriages rather it must be emphasized otherwise unwed fathers will keep fathering children without regard to the deleterious effects on the children. Fatherless boys must be made to discover the peerless value of strong healthy marriages so that history will not repeat itself in their lives and it will be a strong impetus for those aspiring to have good marriages.

Summary

•A happy marriage gives a strong sense of security to children.

•A happy marriage will make a husband spend more time at home and be involved in the lives of his children.

•Prevention of fatherlessness will reduce the incidence of juvenile delinquency.

Points to ponder

•Since a happy marriage does so much good to fathering; in what ways are you tending your marriage so that it stays strong?

•Are involved in the life of your children to the extent that they are developing well?

Further reading

Marcie C Goeke-Morey, E. Mark Cummings. Impact of Father Involvement: A Closer Look at Indirect Effects Models Involving Marriage and Child Adjustment. Applied Developmental Science, Vol 11, Issue 4, Dec.,2007, Pgs 221-225

Back to top

CHAPTER 10 VALUES YOU SHOULD IMPART TO YOUR CHILDREN

At a time of reproductive freedom for women, fatherhood must be more than a matter of DNA. A man must choose to be a father in the same way that a woman chooses to be a mother. ~Mel Feit

Values are cherished societal norms which govern a person's life; they serve as a compass by helping your children navigate the moral chaos of this decadent age. The home was meant to be a bastion of moral values and it was so for many centuries; however today many homes have disintegrated and so cannot provide this vital ingredient for living a successful life. There are many homes that are intact but are totally oblivious of their important role of instilling moral values into their children. Children without values are a liability to society because they live and act without moral restraints. Fathers have the responsibility to teach their children sound moral values that will empower them to make the right choices, when they are alone with their peers.

Many TV programs, internet websites, music, videos, pornographic magazines debase your children's morals. The principal reason why they need to exercise care in what they see and hear is that what you see and hear enter your mind and program you for good or for evil. As a father, you must realize that drugs, alcohol, sex, cultism, pornography are moral traps for today's youths, your mission is to see that your children do not get caught in this web of destruction. An ounce of prevention in this regard is better than a ton of cure. Here are ways to make this wise saying come true for your children:

Teach your children how to make the right choice and how to resist peer pressure. Your children cannot develop in a vacuum; because they have to mix with children who do not share their beliefs, give them pictures of different scenarios and which one to choose when the time comes. Any child can resist peer pressure when he/she is sure he/she is on the right path and when he/she avoids the company of those who do not share his/her convictions.

Teach your children basic ethics and values; do not assume they know on account of what they see you do. Tell your children why telling the truth at all times is a sign of moral rectitude. Tell them how one lie requires many lies to cover its tract, and that every action has repercussion. Share anecdotes and contemporary examples that illustrate what you are teaching them.

Allow your children to learn that some actions are good and some are bad through a reward and punishment system. Reward them for good actions and sanction them for unsavory actions. Empower your children to analyze ethical/ moral issues as you ask them open ended questions such as "why is cheating during examination bad"?

Character

Character is your real nature, a composite of your habits, values and the principles on which you live your life. It is who you are when no one is looking at you. It is what you are made of. It is what is left of you after the shine is gone; there is no make-up that can hide a bad character perpetually. A window into your character is how you treat people who cannot do you any good in return or people who are powerless.

Your character is a description of your behaviour as revealed in the habit of your thoughts and expression, your attitudes and interests, your actions and the personal philosophy of your life.

Truthfulness, integrity, sincerity, trust, fairness, honesty, kindness are all qualities of a person with a good character.

A child's character is determined by:

The family background- His/ her exposure to sound moral instruction from the parents. Children learn so much from what they observe their parents do. Few children rise above the limitations a bad background imposes on them .

The school environment- If the school compliments the home in imparting sound moral instructions he/she would develop a good character. Many schools do not consider character modeling as a top priority; their agenda is to produce excellent academic performance in their students.

The company the child keeps. Good company reinforces good morals while bad company corrupts good morals. Your child must develop the knack of knowing mates who will influence him/her for good and hang out with such.

The choice of books, television programs, films, videos, internet sites a child is exposed to. What a child sees or reads make sensory inputs into the mind of a child which determine how the child behaves.

The personal value system a child adopts early in life. A child can choose to build his/her life on biblical principles early in life. Such a child rejects whatever is contrary to bible stand.

The heroes or heroines in a teenager's life. These persons that have captured your child's imagination have a way of serving as role models for your child. Find out why your child likes such a person and see if there is any good value in that person he/she can model his/her life after.

Self-discipline

Your child needs this virtue to set him/her apart as a responsible adult. No one can achieve any worthwhile goal without self-discipline. Self-discipline is exercising control over every domain of your life.

When a child exercises control over his/her emotions, he/she is able to control his/her temper. The same control is needed over your appetite to prevent gluttony and drunkenness. Social habits such as smoking and use of psychotic drugs are frequently seen in persons who lack discipline. Indisciplined persons also find it difficult to keep to time and this very often undermines their efforts to achieve set goals. You need self-discipline to acquire financial prudence or else you would become a slave to lending institutions.

A child needs self-discipline to be law abiding even when it is not convenient to do so. Without self- discipline a man/woman becomes a slave to his emotions. An adult body with a child's mind is the fitting description of an undisciplined adult.

Delaying gratification

This is the ability to endure hardships in order to achieve set objectives. It entails suffering now so that enjoyment can come later. This trait is discernable in a person most likely to succeed in life. There is always a gestation period for the achievement of most significant things in life and at such periods a person could labour in obscurity, only for him/her to be celebrated publicly for the achievement. Delaying gratification makes sense when you learn to keep your eyes on the future. When you study hard to get good grades, it opens the door for higher paying jobs in future.

Good self- discipline and self- esteem are necessary to acquire this value while a father's caring love helps children to develop this value.

Mental toughness/Personal reinforcement system

This is the inner conviction that makes a person believe that the challenge before him/her is surmountable. Those who snatch victory out of the jaws of defeat usually display this value. They have internalized the aphorism that tough people outlive their tough circumstances because they refused to quit when the going got really tough.

A father needs to teach his children this value because out in the world only the fittest survive and continue to survive. Building this value requires the following:

Self-Belief- You talk yourself into believing that you have all it takes in terms of hard work and acquisition of knowledge to achieve your set goal.

Focus- You have all your internal resources channeled into achieving your set goal.

Tenacity of Purpose/Stick-to-it-iveness- You refused to be intimidated by what you see, hear or feel. Failure only drives you harder in your resolve to succeed at your venture.

Motivation- Change your negative self-talk to positive declaration about the outcome of your project. You program your mind for success with positive affirmation and expectation.

Draw a plan of action and keep to it- Follow every plan of yours to its logical conclusion and change your plans when it is absolutely necessary to do so. Avoid being a "Jack of all trades who is master of none."

See failure as a stepping stone to higher ground-Believe that you are never a failure until you believe you are a failure.

Financial values

"Money matters matter a lot" is an age long saying; you would be doing your child a world of good if you help him/her develop financial intelligence. It does not come naturally to most children; it is a learned act. Consider applying the following measures to help your child acquire this value.

Teach your children to value philanthropy, cultural experiences and personally enriching activities. They should pick up part time jobs as a step to developing a work ethic. Be good savers and disciplined spenders; teach your children that money is not everything. Let your children know that money as medium of exchange is important but it is not an end in itself.

Money is a good servant but a terrible master. Money can be deployed to do many good things in the lives of people, however man has a tendency to worship money because of the security it gives. When all of a man's waking moments is channeled into how to make more money, he can easily be ensnared into doing any evil thing to make money. One of the easiest means of breaking the hold of money over a person's life is by giving it away as philanthropy.

A personal saving culture can be developed when you save at least ten percent of what you earn. Learning to live within your means brings peace to you and saves you from unnecessary hassles.

Learning to meet your debt obligations enables you to build a good credit standing. Spending money on your needs as against your wants would help keep your account in the blue.

Paying your bills as at when due makes you a responsible person.

Summary

•Children brought up with good values are a blessing to society.

•Good character, self-discipline, delaying gratification and mental toughness are values essential for success in life.

•Financial discipline must be taught and modeled to children.

Points to ponder

•What your children observe you do, what you teach them about values as well as the atmosphere at home work together in forming good values in them.

•In what ways do you measure financial discipline to your children? Are you an impulsive buyer or a disciplined spender?

Further reading

William A Belangi. Imparting Values-A multidimensional perspective. Journal of Moral Education, Vol 22, Issue2,1993 pages 111-123

Kool. How to Inculcate Moral Values in Your Child. Available at http://www.gomestic.com/family/How-to-Inculcate-Moral-Values -in-Your-Child/6383/

Back to top

CHAPTER 11 SKILLS YOU SHOULD TEACH YOUR CHILDREN

Do you see a man who excels in his work?

He will stand before kings;

He will not stand before unknown men-Prov. 22:29

Skills are learned activities that confer expertise on a person. When a father equips his children with some of the skills discussed in this chapter, he prepares them to succeed in different endeavours in life. A child's self-confidence gets a boost as he develops new skills. The following skills would make your child stand out among his/her peers if he/she is proficient in them.

Interpersonal skills

These are skills that enable your children get along with others harmoniously. These skills enable them communicate their thoughts and feelings effectively to others as well as enable others give them the expected response. These skills will help their self esteem greatly. The key to developing these skills is appreciating other people and their views, listening to them with undivided attention and giving appropriate answers.

G. K. Chesterton said "The truly great person is the one who makes every person great".

When you treat others with love and respect and listen to them, you will win their respect.

Problem solving skills

A problem is a difficult circumstance or an unresolved issue. Problems and challenges are the lot of man. Things don't often go the way you want them to go. Quite often these challenges are accompanied by stress and suffering. Those who try to avoid problems at all cost and the emotional suffering that goes with it can develop mental illness because they often do not succeed at this goal.

Having problem-solving skills change a person from being a passive recipient of information to being the solution or part of the solution to the problem.

The key to solving a problem is identifying the problem, analyzing it to know its nature and its likely causes while gathering relevant information on it. Some problems can be broken into smaller manageable parts to make solving it easier. This should be followed by exploring all possible options for solving it, choosing an option and then making a plan of action and following it. It is always good to evaluate the result to see if it is satisfactory.

The nature of the problem may range from relationship problems to academic, health, school authorities, law etc

A good rule of thumb in seeking solution to a problem is to always ensure that the solution to your problem is not a problem for another person. When you recognize a problem before it becomes an emergency and act quickly, you spare yourself a lot of headaches.

The only child who never had a problem was the still-born child. Solution to a problem comes from what you know about it and the skills at your disposal in resolving it. Every significant achievement in life comes with a prize; be willing to pay the prize necessary for you to achieve your goals. Always keep in mind that though there may be tears in the night but joy comes in the morning.

Decision making skills

Decision is choosing to act in a particular way on an issue after considering the possible consequences of other choices. You learn to make decision by making decisions on challenges facing you.

Decision making entails risk, making a choice and living with the consequences of your decision. Fear of failure is the commonest reason for indecision.

Teenagers need this skill because they are developing autonomy while being exposed to a bewildering range of choices independent of adults. Some of their decisions can have effects beyond their person such as whether to use drugs, alcohol or cigarettes or to engage in risky behaviour.

The steps to making a decision are listing relevant choices and matching them with their potential consequences. The likelihood of each consequence occurring is assessed while the effect of the possible consequence is deliberated upon before a decision is made. Your child's decision making process is influenced by how he/she reasons, his/her self esteem, what he/she knows about the issue and the influence of his/her peers. Cultural, ethnic and religious beliefs also influence a person's decision making ability.

Adolescents find decision making challenging because they may have only limited options because of inexperience or may be carried away by their emotions and so take unnecessary risks because of inability of estimating the probability of negative consequences.

You will be doing your children a world of good if you are their example in all that is good. Talk with them, listen to their opinions and see how they make decisions on important issues. Allow them make decisions. Be understanding when they make decisions with unfavorable outcomes.

Keep in mind that making decision always for your child on all issues is a prescription for grooming indecisive and immature adults.

Leadership skills

Your children need leadership skills if they are to standout among their peers. While a few persons are born with natural leadership ability, most persons who are aware of its importance must develop this ability. It is generally believed that less than ten percent of a given population has the innate ability to lead.

Leadership is that ability of empowering people to get things done. It requires ideas; time, commitment and faith in people to achieve set goals.

An effective teenage leader needs the following to succeed.

•A vision- Have a picture of what you want to achieve in your mind.

•A mission- A practical way of achieving your goal.

•Good interpersonal skills to enable you win the confidence of those you are working with.

•Self- discipline so that you can exhibit tenacity of purpose.

•Good time management skills.

•Integrity such that people will trust you.

• Good communication skills to enable you present your vision in a way and manner that would generate interest in your followers.

Employment seeking skills

Corporate organizations are always looking out for persons with outstanding skills to hire. When such persons are employed and their skills are well honed, they become an asset to the organization. It is never too early in life to acquaint your children with such skills.

Employers seek:

1.Persons with excellent academic record in a course related to the field in which there is a vacancy. Attending good reputable schools is an added advantage.

2.Good communication skills. You need this to relate well with workers at different levels of hierarchy in your work place.

3.Good interpersonal skills- You need this to get along with your fellow workers as well as with company clients.

4.Good character- Every company looks out for honest workers of integrity who can be trusted with company funds.

5.Capacity for hard work

6.A well groomed appearance. It portrays you as careful and someone who will make a neat representative of the company.

7.Adaptability- Your willingness to handle change in your work environment.

8.Initiative and Independence- Your creativity will empower you to create solution to company problems.

Time management skills

Dost thou love life? Then do not squander time, for that is the stuff life is made of- Benjamin Franklin

Tell me what you think of time and I shall know what to think of you- J.T. Fraser.

Time management is managing your time with a set of practices, principles, tools and skills with the goal of improving the quality of your life through judicious use of time. Your attitude to time reveals your personality type.

Dividends of effective time management

•You will accomplish much within a given time

•You are able to achieve short and long term goals.

•You become disciplined in other areas of your life.

•You have greater balance, fulfillment and satisfactory living.

•You are able to make time for things you want

•You become aware of how you use your time.

Why time is always of the essence

•Teach your child to be a time oriented person, who sets time periods for accomplishing tasks, able to set goals and plan ahead.

•Time is a limited resource; redeeming the time means doing more things within a time period.

•Time management tools include priorities, goals, and planning.

•Time never takes time off-so said Augustine of Hippo

•Create a good pattern in the use of your time

•Time is a gift to gifted purple.

•In the long run it is not the years in your life but the life in your years that count- Adlai Stevenson.

•Time takes on meaning in view of who we are.

Summary

•The world is dominated by people who have skills; equip your children with the skills they need to succeed in life.

•Interpersonal, problem-solving, decision-making, leadership, employment seeking and time management skills are vital skills to be acquired.

Points to ponder

•Make an inventory of the skills your children have, how much of what they have can be attributed to you?

• Skills will open doors for your children; see that your children are equipped with them.

Further reading

Clark, L.S! Help for Parents [2nd Edition]. Parents Press

Back to top

CHAPTER 12 HOW FATHERING AFFECTS CHILDREN'S CAREER CHOICES

My father always told me, "Find a job you love and you'll never have to work a day in your life-Jim Fox

A father leaves indelible impressions on his children by the kind of work he does, whether he likes the job or he is enduring it, how he is rated in his work place, what he says about the job and whether he would like his children to take to the job. A child may follow his/her father's professional footsteps or choose a different career.

A father's parenting style can have a life long effect on the child's career particularly if he acts to boost the child's self-confidence. A strong father-child relationship gives the child a feeling of being loved and a strong sense of security. The effect is life long and it enables the grown child to be open, communicative and trusting of other people. A father's powerful spoken words about his job when internalized by his children often guide their career choice.

Fathers who predetermine the career of their children

There are fathers who because of the exigencies of family business make their children choose certain careers that will make them fit into the family business. Usually such fathers have the wherewithal to give their children the very best in education since the family business stands to gain from it.

Another category of fathers especially professionals like doctors, lawyers, church ministers etc take pride in their careers and often feel delighted to have one of their children take after them. Such children inherit or join their father in his practice. Such professionals will also wish to produce generations of children in that line of profession to make their family unique.

A doctor or lawyer always feels he owes the medical or legal profession a replacement of himself when his time to retire comes.

A third category of fathers chose the career of their children. They are usually sportsmen and sports enthusiasts who believed in their ability to make champions of their children in sports like golf and lawn tennis. Chapter one of this book mentioned the likes of Earl Woods, Richard Williams and Mike Agassi who introduced sports to their children while they were toddlers. They were their children's coaches and they made world champions of them. Some people might wonder if given a choice, these children would have chosen sports as a means of livelihood. Tiger Woods' tribute to his dad who died in 2006 says it all "My dad was my best friend and greatest role model, and I will miss him deeply. I am overwhelmed when I think of all the great things he accomplished in his life. He was an amazing dad, coach, mentor, soldier, husband and friend. I wouldn't be where I am today without him, and I am honoured to continue his legacy of sharing and caring".

How your work experience affects your children

Children who see their Dad dress up leave for work and return later in the day see having a job as a significant achievement in life. They also find it easy to develop good work ethic later in life. They aspire to having gainful employment later in life and are able to relate well with authority figures at work. When a father talks about his career in whatever light, it has a lasting influence on his children. If he talks in a positive exciting light, the children will want to follow in his steps, while if he is full of complaints about the job, the children will not be attracted to his kind of job.

The effect of the job on the father and family also affects the children's career choice. A job that endangers the father's health or life such as working in a mine would not hold any attraction for his children. A job that keeps the father away from home most of the time will be resented by the children.

A father's work ethic affects the children in another way. If he stayed long in a company, they will have the same predisposition when they grow up, because they will consider it normal fare to faithfully serve their employers. Fathers who are not career role models on the other hand may generate anger in their children. That would be a driving force in their rejection of who or what their father was, as a parent and a working adult.

Hard work, ambition and achievement are skills acquired by children from what their father says about his work as well as his attitude to work. Hardworking fathers generally raise hard working sons and daughters through example and communication.

Your relationship with your children affects their career choices

Emotional intelligence which is that ability to have empathy, understanding and insight that promotes social interaction in the workplace can be communicated in a healthy way by a father. This empowers the child to interact well with others in the workplace. Poor interaction at work place may lead to job loss, loss of promotion or frustration at work.

Abusive fathers produce children who are harsh, demanding and unforgiving. Such children who had been hurt seek professions through which they will vent their anger on unsuspecting persons. Hitler and Stalin came from such a background. They were brutalized as children by their fathers; they sought careers in the military and had opportunities to destroy millions of innocent lives.

When children choose a career to please their father

Career choices ordinarily should be based on interests/abilities and job opportunities. Because fathers cast long shadows over the lives of their children; when a father bemoans his inability to pursue a certain career due to unforeseen circumstances earlier in life, some children opt to pursue that career if only to make their fathers happy. This is because verbal and non verbal interaction with children affect what the children think, say and perceive about different vocations. Children go this extra mile for fathers who have been emotionally caring and supportive. Such fathers have provided the child with the inner stamina to cope with what that career demands. The self-esteem, coping skills needed for school, work and social interaction have been developed in the child by the father.

How parents influence the vocational outcome of their children

Parental support and encouragement influence vocational outcome of children. Research has found that when adolescents perceive their father to have high expectations from them, they are likely to have higher aspirations for themselves.

On the other hand, children who never had parental approval and affirmation from their dad while growing up turn out to be adults who in their work places seek the same approval from their boss. This causes friction at the work place because such a worker will be expecting more than his due from the boss.

Passive/absent or over indulgent, guilt driven fathering breeds dependent children who expect their bosses at work to treat them the way their fathers treat them. They keep changing jobs because they are looking for bosses like their fathers.

Other factors which affect a child's career choice

This includes a father's disapproval of his child's career choice. He might do this through statements such as "don't make the same mistakes that I did".

Parent education and income influence a child's career because a rich parent would choose an expensive school for his children because he is likely to get his money's worth in terms of educational outcome for his children. The choice of school, peer influence, the child's personality and ability are also important factors in the child's choice of career. Also parents' occupation and occupational status, as well as parenting style influence the child's vocation.

Family size has been found to be a contributory factor to the child's choice of career because large families tend to have money to put the older children in good schools. As the number of children increase, younger children are affected negatively because the parents put them in schools they can afford not necessarily the school that is the best for them, however they tend to fare better once the financial pressure is less which is usually after the older children have left home.

Summary

•The career of a father and his work experiences affect his children's career choices positively or negatively.

•Some fathers predetermine the career of their children.

•Father-child relationship affects the career choice and vocational outcome of their children

Points to ponder

•What is your influence over your children's career choices?

•Don't try to live your life through your children; match their interest and ability with different careers and guide them to choose the best career for themselves.

Further reading

Parents Talking Career Choices. Available at

http://www.careeradviceaustralia.gov.au

Parents Influence Career Decisions. Crown Financial Ministries. Available at http://www.crown.org/LIBRARY/ViewArticleId=466

Back to top

CHAPTER 13 IMPARTING SEXUALITY EDUCATION TO YOUR CHILDREN

Sometimes the poorest man leaves his children the richest inheritance. ~Ruth E. Renkel

It is important you teach your children about the changes that are occurring in their bodies during adolescence. Lack of this basic knowledge about human sexuality exposes them to misleading information about this aspect of their lives. In the United States alone, there about one million teenage pregnancies and three million cases of sexually transmitted diseases each year. If these figures are projected for the rest of the world, the number becomes staggering and it becomes easy to appreciate the value of talking to your children about their sexuality. In the developing countries, death from unsafe abortions is one of the significant causes of maternal mortality; children must be told of the consequences of certain behaviours.

A lot of children that end up in trouble do so when they get over stimulated from exposure to indecent films, internet sites and literature that are inappropriate for them.

When a father through open, honest and regular communication talk about sex and sexuality, the choices you make and their consequences, it helps youngsters learn about sex in a healthy and positive manner from a significant person they trust.

Why it is your responsibility to instruct your child on this issue:

•Your rights and duties as a father are irreplaceable and inalienable on sensitive issues like this and so you cannot entirely delegate it to others, unless physical illness or absence makes it impracticable.

•You are the most credible person in your children's life; they would believe whatever you say on this issue.

•Adolescence brings in its wake, interest in the opposite sex; you can answer their questions in an open and truthful way.

•For your daughter, in the absence of her mother, you can get a female whom your daughter has confidence in and who is knowledgeable and shares your conviction on such issues to talk to her on the changes going in her body.

•When you talk to your children on this issue, you close the door to their learning about their sexuality from their peers. Peers very often misled their friends on this issue because they lack accurate knowledge of what is going on in their bodies.

•Discussion on this subject will strengthen the bond between you and your children.

•Each of your children is unique and must receive individualized education. You know what each child needs in this area and you aim to meet each child's needs.

•You have the right to educate your children in conformity with your moral and religious convictions.

When to start sexuality education

This depends on when the child's curiosity is aroused and on such occasion you should limit your answer to the child's question. Let the scope of your answer be within what the child can comprehend. Overloading the child with too much information that is not necessary and beyond comprehension only breeds confusion.

At puberty, the physical changes that herald the onset of puberty make it imperative for you to talk about this issue to your adolescents.

How to give sexuality education

1.Make the discussion a dialogue to provide freedom for your child to ask questions.

2.Be open in sharing your values and concerns. You may use anecdotes and current happenings where necessary to drive home your points.

3.Keep the discussion simple and age appropriate. Find out words that your child uses for that part of the body and use them in your explanation. This has a way of putting your child at ease.

4.Keep in mind the cultural context in which you live.

5.Do not display any form of shame during the discussion so that your child will not associate sexuality with shame.

6.Discuss the importance of responsibilities for choices and decisions you make about this aspect of life. The pros and cons of decisions must be evaluated for all decisions. Relate sex to love, intimacy, caring and respect for one's self and partner.

7.Graphic details should be avoided.

8.Books that use illustration or diagrams that aid communication could be made available to the child.

9.Getting advice from a pediatrician, a family physician or any healthcare practitioner when you are at a loss about what to say is very helpful. It guarantees the accuracy of what you are saying.

What to teach

•Teach what the next few years of puberty will bring about; the physical and psychological changes that typify this phase of life. They need to know that these changes are only for a short time; however how they cope with them determines if they would evolve to be well adjusted adults.

•Teach the morality and responsibility of sex in an age appropriate manner.

•Explain what self- control measures in this regard entails- e.g. Discipline of the senses, the mind, what they read, what they watch and the kind of company they keep.

•Explain what boundaries around relationships are. Teach assertiveness in dealing with sexually-oriented advances.

•Teach on gender roles and how to develop valuable skills.

•Teach that chastity before marriage means that a person values his/her body as a meaningful gift to the spouse

•Teach on the sanctity of sex. It is meant for marriage and not for entertainment.

•Teach on relationship skills.

•Teach on what is/ what is not appropriate to watch on the TV.

•Present modern positive role models and talk of what youngsters can emulate from them.

•Teach on appropriate dressing that emphasizes modesty.

Benefits of sexuality education

•Fosters parent- child relationship. Your child confidently approaches you on issues bothering him/her in this aspect of life.

•Prepares your child to face the challenges of the future. Your child would be forewarned about wolves out there and the need to be careful.

•Helps delay the onset of sexual activity till marriage.

•Helps reduce the chances of unplanned pregnancy and sexually transmitted diseases.

•Increases true knowledge of human sexuality among teenagers.

•It empowers the youth to assert him/herself in the face of a sexually-oriented situations.

•It fosters respect and responsibility.

•It helps in the prevention of HIV/AIDS.

•It helps the young person to define boundaries around his/her relationships.

•It promotes social maturity and reduces incidence of problems related to dating and sexuality.

Summary

•Sexuality education is teaching children about the changes that occur in the body during the adolescent phase of life.

•It is one of the duties of a father to instruct his children on this issue.

•There are many benefits to instructing children about their sexuality.

Points to ponder

•A lot of fathers shy away from this topic; however they must know that problems arising from this aspect of life can have dire consequences.

•Start talking to your children about their sexuality and what they need to do to handle it in a healthy way.

Further reading

"Talk To Me"-Sexuality Education for Parents: Public Health Agency of Canada. Available at http://www.phac-aspc.gc.ca/publicat/cgshe-Idnemss/index-eng.php

Back to top

CHAPTER 14 THE DIVORCED FATHER

It is easier for a father to have children than for children to have a real father. ~Pope John XXIII

The need for a divorced father to recover from the trauma of divorce cannot be over emphasized. So many things are at stake that call for attention. While you cannot unscramble an egg, it can be turned into an omelet. There are lots of fathers especially those brought up in foster homes who have no idea of how to be a good parent because they never had one themselves; a loving father would not want to bequeath a fatherless legacy to his children. How can a divorced father care for himself so that the consequences of divorce on himself and his children will be mitigated is the subject of this chapter.

The pains of the divorced father come from the following:

•Shattered dreams- a once solid family that has disintegrated conjures feelings of failure in a man and this can make him retreat into himself. A study found divorced men in the age range of 20 to 60 years to have 70%-100% higher rates of death than married men. Be determined to outlive your marital challenges.

•Chronic grief arising from disengagement with his children whom he had been close to before divorce. The father must resolve this grief, adapt to his child's physical absence, to the loss and be reconciled to his visiting status in his child's life.

•The need to adopt a help seeking behaviour to overcome grief. He must come to terms with the reality of his situation instead of living in denial.

•The legal wrangling that goes with custody rights and access to children after divorce. Lawyers often escalate the estrangement after divorce in a bid to make their services invaluable.

•Payment of child support could be challenging to some fathers while failure to pay can lead to incarceration.

Advantages of keeping in touch with your children

Children in almost all cases of divorce did not play any part in the breakup of their parents yet the consequences are borne by them nonetheless. A father must do all he can to protect his children especially knowing that they are innocent in the matter. A father's involvement in the life of his children after divorce has the following effects:

•It prevents clinical depression, eating disorders and anxiety in daughters who are separated from their fathers following divorce.

•Research has found that boys who have little or no relationship with their fathers especially if their mother did not remarry tend to be more aggressive, socially immature, exhibit more behavioral problems which pitch them against the law.

•Girls who grow up with single mothers grew up too fast by dating, having sex or getting married at an early age. This is because divorced mothers tend to give more freedom to their children to make up for the absence of their father. At the other end of the spectrum are girls who because of their parents divorce become extremely uncomfortable with dating and relationship with males.

•Teenage children who maintain close contact with their dads do better in their studies because their Dad encourages them to have higher educational goals.

•Self- reliance, self-discipline and self- motivation are values children depend on their fathers for. He teaches them these values.

Reasons why divorced fathers lose touch with their children

•Many divorced fathers stopped seeing their children because of the volatile relationship they have with their children's mother. They either want to avoid a fight and conflict or the mothers deny them access. A father should maintain his cool despite provocation so that access to his children will not be denied.

•Some men stop seeing their children because they do not know how to care for a child and don't want to look stupid.

•Men with jobs are more likely to be involved in their children's lives than men without jobs. Jobless men feel worthless and unable to contribute to their children's lives until they get a job. Community service society reported that in New York City, only 51.9% of black men aged 16 to 64 were employed.

•The problems of distance, transportation, poor finances, work schedule or lack of accommodation are secondary factors in preventing fathers from maintaining contact with their children.

What premarital counsel can a father give his children?

•Tell them to be determined not to repeat their parents mistakes. When you choose to marry, get a partner who has very strong beliefs in the institution of marriage. The divorce industry is strong and thriving because it enjoys government patronage in some parts of the world, try not to be caught in its web.

•Do not rush into marriages or relationships. It's been found that persons who delay marriage till they are between 22 and 27 years have better marital outcomes. Ensure you are physically, emotionally and materially prepared for marriage.

•Strive to develop effective relationship skills.

•Develop a strong sense of being your own person whether or not in a relationship.

•Ensure financial security prior to marriage and before having children.

Coping with divorce

•You need the support of your family and friends. When you have a strong support of networks of family and friend, they make you feel you are not alone in this crisis.

•Do not make the children take sides, keep line of communication with them open. They need both of you to survive.

•Do not prolong the legal process of divorce to minimize the trauma to all the parties and preserve your relationship with your children.

Summary

•A divorced father must come to terms with the reality of his situation and make moves to mitigate the effect of the divorce on his life and children. There is life after divorce.

•There are many advantages in staying in touch with your children after divorce.

•A divorced father needs the support of his family and friends to cope with the situation.

Points to ponder

•When last did you set your eyes on your children after your marriage broke up?

•What are you doing to mitigate the effects of divorce on your children?

•Do all within your power to meet your financial obligations to your children.

Further reading

Wayne Parker. Top 7 Keys for Success as a Divorced Dad. Available at http://www.fatherhood.about.com/od/divorceddads/tp/divorced_dads

Back to top

CHAPTER 15 PREPARING YOUR CHILDREN FOR MARRIAGE

Why are men reluctant to become fathers? They aren't through being children. ~Cindy Garne

In most cultures, a father gives the daughter's hand in marriage to commence the wedding ceremony; actually this should be the last step in a process that would have started in the child's teenage years. A father has a duty in telling his daughter what she needs to know about men so that she can make informed decision on what kind of man to marry. His input into his son's marriage preparation is in the area of telling him what kind of preparation precedes marriage; this also should start in the teenage years. Marriage is one institution that requires a father's input; just as in a relay race, successful exchange of batons is one of the determinants of who wins the race, so a proper exchange of information in this sphere of life aids children in making the right choices. It is good for children to know that preparing themselves to be the right marriage partner is as important as getting the right spouse for themselves.

Good personal preparation for marriage and good choice of partner predict good marital outcome

First time marriages are more likely to succeed than subsequent marriages. In the US, first time marriages that end in divorce last an average of 11 years for both men and women. Remarriages ending in divorce last an average of 7.4 years for men and 7.1 years for women. Nationally, all marriages ending in divorce in America last an average of 9.8 years.[for more data go to www.divorceinfo.com/statistics.htm]. A judge that was overcome with curiosity as to why after 68 years of marriage, an elderly couple was seeking divorce was told: "we were waiting for the children to die".

One way of preparing your children for marriage is to look at the causes of divorce and start preparing them to look at such factors in themselves and their future partners with a view to avoiding such pitfalls. Quality of premarital relationship, partner's relationship styles, poor communication, lack of commitment, and infidelity are some of the commonest causes of divorce.

One recent analysis of divorce cases found the causes to be: Extramarital Affairs-27%, Family Strains/Misunderstanding-18%, Abuse [Physical and emotional]-17%, Addiction to drugs and alcohol-13%, Mid-life Crisis-13%, Workaholism-6%, others-6%. With the above data, it is obvious that much of what causes divorce has to do with emotional maturity. Preparation in this realm helps you recognize who you would be happy with in marriage.

Check list for your children as they grow up

Biological maturity has to do with chronological age and physical size that can cope with challenges in marriage. It is necessary that a person be biologically mature for marriage because it has a bearing with psychological and social maturity [preparedness for marriage].

Studies have found persons who married between the ages of 23 and 27 to have better outcome than those who married in their teenage years.

Parents can coach their children to attain emotional maturity and this can be assessed by the presence of the following qualities in their children:

Self-Acceptance God made you a unique original person, don't settle for an imitation. When you accept yourself with your strengths and limitations people come to like you that way. Of course, there is room for continual improvement especially in the area of emotional maturity. A person who lacks self-acceptance will find it difficult to accept other persons the way they are.

Self-Control This is the product of self-discipline that helps you control your passions, emotions and desires. Persons who are garrulous, indiscreet, abuse alcohol and substances and have extramarital affairs lack self-control. A person who has self-control can easily pick it in a person who lacks it. It is one of the qualities of a mature person.

Wisdom This is the uncanny ability of knowing what to do in many situations. You get wisdom from applying what you know, by learning from your experience and other peoples' experience. It enables you to make quick decisions and solve problems as they arise in life.

A Sense of Responsibility This means you can be depended upon, you are accountable for your actions, finances and work habits. It means you can be trusted.

Self-Esteem This is the inner strength that comes from self confidence in your ability to succeed at any task you work upon. It makes you enjoy your life. People like you when you have this quality because you do not pose any threat to them; you are not unnecessarily touchy.

Independence You are your own person and not tied to the apron strings of your parents. You are able to make decisions and the face consequences. Marriage entails leaving your parents and cleaving to your spouse to build your family.

Counsel to your daughter regarding the choice of a suitor

A father is in a good position to prepare his daughter to enable her make a good choice of a husband. The following points are worth discussing with your daughter:

His christian beliefs are very important. What does Christ mean to him, is he a child of God? Has the Bible a strong hold over his life? What commitment does he have in his church? The longest bible passage on marriage can be found in Ephesians 5:22-33; it clearly spells out the role of the husband and wife in the relationship. Only committed Christians take their biblical roles in marriage seriously.

A man may find you sexually attractive but may not have real love for you. Real love is the only basis for life long relationship. A man who pesters you for sex early in a relationship has no self control and may be unfaithful after marriage. What he is exhibiting is infatuation, the very antithesis of real love.

What is his perception of marriage? Do you share the same convictions that marriage is for life? Does he want to play safe by asking for cohabitation? Divorce rate is higher in couples who got in to marriage through cohabitation.

Is he affectionate? Does he demonstrate affection readily? In his relationship with others is he loving? Love is such that it cannot be limited to one's intended spouse. A husband's number one duty is to love his wife and this love is measured by the amount of sacrifice he is willing to make for his wife.

Are you compatible with him in your daily habits, do you share the same values and priorities in life? You will find this out with pointed questions or as he reacts to situations around him.

How developed are his communication skills, men talk more during courtship and there is no better way of settling marital conflicts than through dialogue. A man who cannot share his feelings may be hard to live with and difficult to please.

How developed is his sense of empathy? Does he have emotional self awareness? Is he able to sense when another person is sad and offer some kind words? A husband would need to exercise a lot of this virtue in marriage.

Is he a very intentional person? Does he say what he means and mean what he says? Prevarication or chronic inability to make up one's mind can be a challenging problem in marriage because the husband has a duty to lead the family. Family leadership is mostly about making decisions.

Is a sense of commitment his strong point? What responsible positions has he held so far in his church or work place? Is he an accountable person who readily offers motives for his actions? Does he have the stamina to work through challenging situations? Marriage offers very many challenges which will require decisive actions on the part of the husband.

Does his temperament suit yours; is he an optimist or pessimist? Optimists are easier to live with because they are easily pleased. Optimists live longer, achieve more in life and enjoy better health.

Is he resilient? Does he have that ability to bounce back after a reversal of fortune? How does he manage adverse events? Are his shock absorbers good? Marriage has its ups and downs; a man should be ready at all times to face up to challenges.

Is he good at managing his anger or does he blow his top at the slightest provocation? How does he respond to your anger; does he calm you down or does he escalate it?

Does he exhibit balance in his life? Is he good at combining learning, work and leisure in his daily life? Workaholism on the part of the husband has wrecked many promising marriages.

How does he adapt to change? Does he calmly accept what he cannot change or does he escape into denial when the unexpected happens?

A man's background is either an asset or a liability to him. It is an asset if he comes from a two parent home where he has seen marriage lived out in the Christian context. If the fathering he had was the authoritative type, he will most probably pass same down to his children. Having educated parents reduces their chances of interfering in his marriage. On the other hand, a man from a fatherless home [single parent home for whatever cause] and none Christian background would find it hard to give what he never had. Unless he has had a significant male figure who had mentored him while growing up and unless he had read and attended marriage seminars to make up for his deficiencies; marriage to him will be challenging.

No man has all the above listed qualities, however the more of these qualities a man has, the better a husband material he will be.

Counsel to your son

The husband is the head of the home according to Judeo-Christian tradition [Eph 5:22-33]. Every family is limited by the type of leadership the husband provides. A husband who utilizes all his energy and emotional resources to source for money would sentence his family to mediocrity. A real man must consider these aspects of his life before going into marriage:

Spiritual Maturity- He must be enjoying an intimate personal relationship with Christ evidenced by a good prayer life and consistent reading of the Bible. Church involvement is also a vital aspect of spiritual maturity and an evidence of commitment to the Lord.

Are you sufficiently prepared to be a blessing to the lady you wish to marry? The authority you would wield as a husband is expressed in love when you provide, clothe, shelter and protect your wife. Are you emotionally mature to be a husband? Do you have self-control? Do you accept reality or you choose to live in dreams? How do you cope with loses and regrets? Do you make decisions readily? How are your problem-solving skills, are they above average? Are you disciplined as regards finances? How do you manage anger? Poor control over anger can mark you out as a potential wife abuser. In what areas do you need to develop yourself further? Can you hold yourself in integrity in an atmosphere of conflicts and compromise? How do you face challenges? Do you hide from them or you seek solutions to them promptly? What are your work habits; are you taken seriously at work, are you a stickler for professional excellence? How good are you at sustaining relationships? Are your communication skills good? Do you have inspirational mentors that you want to pattern your life after? Are you growing in wisdom concerning the things of God?

Choice of lady to marry

The realities on the ground especially with regard to the burgeoning divorce industry calls for restraint in choosing who to marry. The following aspects of a lady's life would be a pointer to her suitability:

Deep personal relationship with the Christ that is characterized by sound prayer life and consistent reading of the Bible. Active participation in the life of a church is indicative of commitment. A Christian perspective on marriage that believes marriage is for life and must be worked upon daily for the good of the partners as well as their offsprings.

A lady of good character that values integrity, honesty, hard work and faithfulness should be your desire; somebody of a quiet and gentle spirit, not quarrelsome or cantankerous.

Someone whose temperament is compatible and complimentary with yours and who has a lot in common with you on morals and values. Someone who cherishes traditional family values.

A woman's background is an asset if she comes from a two parent Christian family where an authoritative fathering style was in operation. If she comes from a single parent home [whatever the cause of this family situation], you will need to ensure you have convergence of perception about marriage before proceeding.

Encounter with a suitor

A father who has a daughter invariably will meet his child's suitor before giving his consent. Some fathers may not know what to say while some experienced dads have no problems here. A father at all times will seek to protect his daughter's interest and in doing this he might need to chat with the suitor after welcoming him with an open with mind.

Ask him about his age, educational background and family background. What are his Christian beliefs particularly as pertains to marriage? Does he have an opt-out clause in his marriage beliefs or he believes marriage is for life?

Ask him why he has decided to ask for your daughter's hand in marriage? What are the things in her that made him feel she is the right person for him?

What are his interests, what significant posts/offices has he held at school, workplace or church that can reveal something about his character?

Has he been married before and if yes what caused the divorce? Has he been involved in courtship before, if yes what caused the breakup?

What personal preparations has he made to ensure he has a good marriage? Has he read books or attended marriage seminars?

Has he any role model he wants to model his marriage after? This will give you an insight into what he appreciates in marriage.

Summary

•You have the important duty of preparing your son or daughter for marriage because a good choice of a spouse guarantees good marital outcome.

•It is good to have a checklist of values your children ought to have as they approach the age of marriage.

•It is good to counsel them about what to look out for in a potential life partner.

Points to ponder

•This is perhaps the most important role you would play in the adult life of your child. If your child makes the right decision in this all important issue of life, you will enter into your rest concerning your child.

•You can only imagine the consequences of a wrong decision at this phase of life; help your child make the right decision.

Further reading

Barbara H. Cross. Preparing Your Children for Marriage. Available at http://www.homepage.ntlworld.com/haylett/fm/fmII_marriage.html

Family Ministry-Preparing Your Children for Marriage. Available at http://www.trinitywa.com/transcripts/Preparing_Your_Children_for_Marriage

Howard Hendricks. Child Rearing-Preparing Young People for Marriage. Santa Ana, CA: Vision House Publishers, 1971

Back to top

CHAPTER 16 CHALLENGES OF YOUTHS IN THE 21ST CENTURY

Youth can be characterized as a transition from childhood to adulthood-a developmental journey during which one gains independence and begins to participate fully in society. This period is fraught with enormous challenges for young people themselves and for the rest of society. It is imperative that societies invest in their youths, as they are especially vulnerable to the increasingly complex problems facing the world today. United Nations World Youth Report 2003

Dad your guiding hand on my shoulder will remain with me forever-Author Unknown

The present generation of youths is facing more complex challenges than the previous generations and they need the guiding hand of their fathers to surmount these challenges.

The World Youth Report of 2005 described in details challenges facing youth with the goal of galvanizing nations to take action to help youths. The UN definition of youth encompasses young men and women in the age bracket of 15 to 24 years. People in this age bracket are characterized by ample energy, enthusiasm, idealism and creative abilities that can be channeled into useful ends. Unfortunately, many nations have failed to effectively and systematically integrate issues of young people into national programmes. Most of such programmes are still add-ons and in small scale so that their effects are limited. Individual families must take up the slack in bridging the divide between national efforts and family efforts to help young people.

A father's response to youth issues

A father as the head of the home can benefit from the World Youth Report by preparing his children to meet these challenges. A plan of action for each child can be drawn based on the perceived needs of his child in the areas identified by the World Youth Report.

The ten priority areas are education, employment, hunger and poverty, health, environment, drug abuse, juvenile delinquency, leisure time activities, girls and young women and participation of youth in the life of society. The UN Secretary General's World Report of 2005 noted that 18% of the world's population are in age groups 15 to 24yrs and more than 75% of them live in the developing world.

A father can prepare his children for these challenges in the following areas:

•Education The emphasis is on high quality education. Good education promotes mastery of the subject as against just passing examination. Good education also conditions a child for life-long learning. You are the most important determinant of the educational outcome of your child- See chapter 8 of this book on how you can enhance your child's learning ability

•Youth Employment According to the International Labour Organization. " compared to adults, young people today are more than three times as likely to be unemployed......(and) being without a job which means being without a chance to work themselves out of poverty". For your children to have a real chance to find decent and productive work, they must be employable, have entrepreneurial skills that would help them to be self-employed. Employment skills were discussed in Chapter 11 of this book.

•Leisure Activities These range from helpful extra- curricular activities such as sports and music to activities that threaten youth well-being such as risky sexual behaviour, delinquency, substance abuse and criminal tendencies. Prowess in sports can provide gainful employment as mentioned in chapter 1 of this book and fathers can play a significant role in this. Risky sexual behaviours can be prevented when fathers apply the measures outlined in chapter 6 of this book. Delinquency, substance abuse, criminal behaviours are very rampant in fatherless homes. Fathers who are actively involved in the lives of their children minimize this risk. Time spent on TV and Internet should be curtailed while the contents of what they watch should be censored. Violent films and sexually explicit movies and pornography debase the child's mind and prime him/her for self-destructive lifestyles.

•Environment Youths are sensitive to environmental issues because they feel destroying the environment leaves them with a bleak future. Part of the crisis in the Niger Delta of Nigeria had been youth militancy triggered by the vast environmental degradation caused by oil exploration in the region. A father can influence the child away from joining militant groups to participating in advocacy groups that draw the world's attention to the plight of youths in this region.

•Volunteer Service/Work This contributes to social cohesion by empowering excluded sections of society so that their sense of self- worth is enhanced. Participants imbibe a commitment to change which translates into initiation of new ventures after the service experience. Encourage your children to participate in volunteer services, it adds to their curriculum vitae and gives them a competitive edge when they go for job interviews.

•Health Youths evolve from protected childhood to independent adulthood. Youth can be a stage of transitional risk behaviour like delinquency, sexual escapades, experimentation with harmful substances, pornography. HIV and AIDS affect youth more than any other segment of the world's population.

Teenage pregnancy affects mother and child's health, impairs girls' education and marriage prospects.

Smoking is the leading cause of preventable deaths in the world Alcohol intake is a big threat to youth lives in many countries of the world.

Criminal activities The World Youth Report noted that statistically young people constitute the most criminally active segment of the population, although eventually most will desist from criminal and deviant activities. In most cases the offenders are males acting in groups. Young people are also disproportionately the victims of crime and violence.

Pending when nations will make solutions to youth problems a prominent item on their agenda, fathers should hold the forth and work to see that their children come out unscathed through this myriad of challenges.

Summary

•Youths are facing complex challenges that parents must know about and prepare their youths to overcome.

•The world youth report has highlighted the problem areas that fathers can look into.

Points to ponder

•In what ways are you involved in the life of your youth to prepare him or her for the challenges that lie ahead?

•Take care of your youth today so that he/she can take care of you in old age.

Further reading

Fabrice Lehman: The Challenges of Youth in the 21st Century. Is Globalization the Answer? Available at
http://www.ku.edu.tr/files/corporate/owl-Istanbul-final%20report.pdf

Youth Challenges in Today's Society: Introduction. Available at
http://www.highbeam.com/doc/IGI-139049294html

##########

Thank you for reading my book. If you enjoyed it, please take a moment and leave a review at your favorite retailer.
Thanks
Francis Edo Olotu

Back to top

ABOUT THE AUTHOR

Dr Francis Edo Olotu is a 1979 graduate of the University of Lagos Medical School, Nigeria He is the medical director of Christ Hospital, Ondo which he founded 25 years ago. He combines his private medical practice with marriage and family counseling. He has been a leader in the Catholic Charismatic Renewal of Nigeria for over three decades. He speaks often at seminars and conferences on themes that center on the Christian family as well as Life in the Spirit. He has a passion for fathers and believes their role in the family cannot be outsourced. He is the convener of the Purpose Driven Fathers Network based in Ondo as well as an author of books and articles to inspire fathers. Dr Olotu is the Editor of the Nigerian Journal of General Practice. His other books are *Releasing the Power in Fatherhood, Help for Parents! Maximized Parenting:112 Solutions to the Parenting Problems of Today[Co-authored with Catherine Olubukunola Olotu] and Your Guide to Cancer Prevention: Risk Factors, Early Detection Tests and Preventive Measures for 25 Common Cancers*. He is married to Catherine and the union is blessed with four children.

A CHAPTER FROM MY NEW BOOK: MAXIMIZED PARENTING:112 SOLUTIONS TO THE PARENTING PROBLEMS OF TODAY

Necessary Skills for Parenting

What are the necessary skills for parenting?

There are no skills required for fathering or conceiving a child if both parents are physically healthy; however parenting a child needs an assortment of skills to ensure good outcomes for the child at different stages of his/her life. Good parenting gives a child a head start in life and prepares him or her to grab every opportunity that comes across his/her path to succeed in life. Parenting skills are not taught in any school as a subject; however any person who had a good upbringing and attended a good school knows by experience what to do in raising a child. Parenting seminars or workshops and joining parental support groups are other avenues where a parent can update his or her skills. Reading good books on family, marriage and parenting are good sources of knowledge about children and how to help them develop successfully.

The ability to love and express affection is critical at every stage of raising a child. Knowledge of your child-his likes, dislikes, strengths and weaknesses helps in training your child. You need to be safety conscious as a parent of a toddler and ensure the child plays within your sight's range. Keep medications, sharp objects and dangerous fluids like shoe polish or kerosene which a child can drink out of the child's reach. Ensure electricity sockets not in use are sealed off with tapes to avoid a child sticking metal objects into them and getting electrocuted. Ensure your child gets to play with adequate toys since children learn through play at this stage of life. Observe your child to know if his/her developmental milestones are appropriate for the age and see a pediatrician if you are not satisfied with his/her growth and development. Ensure your child gets all the vaccinations appropriate for his/her age. It is good to know how your child looks and behaves in good health so that every departure from what is normal is attended to promptly. Pediatricians have advised that children under the age of 2 should not watch television while children under 5 should be restricted to less than 2 hours of television viewing a day. It has been found that excessive watching of television by children under 5 leads to poor development of social and communication skills because such children do not spend enough time interacting with people, an activity from which they would learn the skills.

Place a high premium on education beginning from the preschool days so that your child will take learning as a part of life. Schedule a time for learning in the home for your child. This is the time to teach your child some values like learning to greet, learning to say "thank you", learning to say "I am sorry" et cetera. Give your child age-appropriate responsibility at home such as setting the table for meals, picking up her toys and returning them to her toy box after play. Keeping an eye on your child's nutrition early in life has a positive bearing on his/her future health because some illnesses like obesity have their roots early in life from inappropriate diet. As a parent you should teach your child how to greet people according to your culture and how to show respect for elders and authority figures. When it comes to discipline, be consistent in delivering on your promises for bad or for good behavior. Set limits to your child's behavior regarding what is acceptable behavior at home, school and elsewhere. Communicate your expectation; tell your child what misconduct is in an age-appropriate way. Model this particular behavior to your child. For a preschool child, drawing on the wall can be misbehavior or tearing a furniture covering. Be your child's role model; use role play to make your child think in advance. You will be helping him develop a more thoughtful and flexible response to the everyday problems he may face. Pay compliments to your child when he acts well according to instructions.

Getting to know your child's friends and their background is important because they will influence your child with time. Guiding your child in his/her choice of friends will help your child conform to your instructions because bad company corrupts good morals. Teaching and communication skills are vital to parenting. For adolescent/teenagers, you need to train them to be caring, independent and responsible adults. Give your child age-appropriate sexuality education. Stay connected by making out time to do things with your teenager; in such informal settings you, will be opportuned to hear him talk about his hopes, aspirations and challenges and this will give you a chance to offer him/her advice. Be very positive in your dealing with your teenager and for every reprimand, ensure you pay three compliments. Allow your teenage child some degree of self-expression in clothes and hairstyle; tell him/her about the dangers of extreme fashion fads like tattooing and body piercing. Warn your teenager about the dangers of the internet; tell him not to disclose personal information on the internet. Train your child to shun premarital sex. Learn to be specific when setting curfew, instead of telling your teen not to stay out late, give him/her a specific time to be home.

As your child becomes more responsible, be flexible and grant him/her more freedom; if he/she shows poor judgment, impose more restrictions. Put your rules in writing to counter selective amnesia by your child. Be willing to explain your decisions to your child; be reasonable, do not set rules your child cannot keep. Prioritizing rules helps you and your teenager negotiate and reach compromise. Subjects over which you can negotiate are home work habits, food choices, TV watching, internet use and bed time. Do not negotiate on things that border on your teen's safety such as substance abuse, sexual activity and reckless driving. Enforce consequences for actions that are against your laid down rules; always let your child know you are a parent and not a pal. Your child has only two parents and their job description is well laid out but he/she can have as many friends as he/she wants. When you are too lenient with infractions against your rules, your child sees you as not serious; while being too harsh brings resentment. Active ignoring can be employed in handling your teen when what he/she is boiling over is inconsequential.

Scold or reprimand your teen's misbehavior not his person; do not use demeaning words and do not do it when his friends are present. Imposing additional household chores can be an additional punishment when he commits a punishable offense. Imposing additional restriction can also serve as punishment or taking away privileges like phone use. Asking your teen to suggest consequences for breaking rules might make him more disposed to accepting punishment if he breaks rules. Be a positive example to him in all you want to be.

Improving communication with your child

Effective communication is a two way process where one party speaks in a way the other party understands what he is saying and responds appropriately. Communication is at the heart of parenting; your child must understand what you are saying to him appropriately. Words are very powerful; they have the power to build as well as the power to destroy. When used creatively in parenting, you are able to shape the lives of children positively. The bible in Proverbs 18:21 says, "Death and Life are in the power of the tongue and those who love it will eat its fruit". Words are likened to seeds which germinate when planted and bear fruits; ensure the words spoken into your child's life are such that will bear positive fruit in the child. The bible in Colossians 4:6 also says, "Let your speech always be with grace, seasoned with salt, that you may know how you ought to answer each one" Children have a future and parents are significant determinants of their children's future.

I remember, a lady who came for medical treatment in my clinic and in passing mentioned that her husband constantly makes reference to different things his Dad told him about life. She regretted that her father was never home in her formative years due to his job and so she could not remember anything he told her about life. My wife once asked my son, if he remembered my instructions to him during his boarding house years. To use his words, he answered "I remember Dad's words as if a recorder is playing them back to me". There is a parent voice in every child that retains valuable instructions about life that parents have passed on to their children; ensure that there is a rich deposit of words of wisdom from you to your child as he grows up. Children are to be nurtured and loved through words and actions. Good communication is essential for parent-child bonding and also for transmission of knowledge and wisdom that would make your child grow in maturity.

Instructions should be explicit and consistent while your child should feel loved and feel it is for his/her own good that you are speaking. Get close physically to your child while talking; use your child's first name to personalize the instruction such as, "Charles, I want you to empty the trash bin first thing in the morning". Keep your instructions positive; like "Tidy your room before you go to school" instead of "Do not leave your room in a mess while you go to school". When speaking to your child, the tone of your voice, your gestures and facial expression determine how he/she will receive the instruction. Give your child room to respond after an instruction in case there is a need for clarifications about what you just said. Instructions should be kept simple with two or three subjects in a sentence such as "Mary, get your laundry done before watching the television" rather than lengthy sentences containing diverse instructions which may appear confusing to your child.   Maintain eye contact with your child while he/she is talking and tell him/her you believe what he/she is saying. When you are giving instructions about the differences between right and wrong, let your expression reveal concern for the well being of your child.

Communicate in a way that depicts respect; and when there is a communication problem it is safe to assume the problem is from your end; always take into consideration your child's mood and choose when best to communicate. Be aware of the surrounding when talking so that your child would not be embarrassed. Allow him room to ask questions so that uncertainties would be clarified from his/her mind. Find time each week for a one on one activity with your child and learn about his/her interests. In relating with your children; listen to what they are saying-this makes them feel honored. Avoid bad labels such as "You always waste time", instead give good labels such as "Son, you are improving in your time-keeping ability". Teach positive self talk such as "I am an overcomer". Focus on their goals and how you will help them achieve their goal. When a child errs, ask what he has learned from his mistake; when you talk from this perspective, he/she feels honored and more likely to listen to your word of wisdom.

Initiate conversation with your child by sharing on what is on your mind about an issue or by asking open-ended questions such as "Tell me the exciting and not so exciting things that happened in your day today". Take seriously whatever scares or embarrasses him and try to allay his fears. Informal settings are best for communicating with your child such as when taking your child to school or church, at dinner time, during a family game of scrabble or monopoly, while taking a walk as exercise. You can tell stories about your childhood or discuss events that happened in your place of work with your child. Teach your child not to interrupt others while they are talking. You can ask your child to give you a narrative about a recent movie they watched on television. Teach him to say "please" when asking for a favor and "thank you" when it is granted him.

Listening is important to your child- give undivided attention without being intrusive. Resist interrupting your child. Repeat what you heard to ensure that you understood what they said. Respond gently to your child's questions because angry or defensive response would make him tune you out. Let your child know your opinion even if it is contrary to his. Let your child know he has the right to disagree, but ensure you explain your position clearly without hurting his feelings. When you turn down a request, explain why it is so. Talk to; but don't lecture, criticize or say hurtful things to your children. Kids learn from their own choices. Your child may tell you only a bit of what he is upset about; listen attentively and encourage him to share the whole story. Be generous with compliments over every little achievement of your child and hug your child as often as possible. Buy gifts very often for your children, it communicates value to them.

Listening to your child is time well invested

Listening is a learned skill; it is an important part of communication which enables you to know what is going on in the mind of your child. By listening, you will discover what challenges your child is facing, how he is coping and what assistance you can give him. Listening is one of the building blocks of lasting relationship with your child. Listening conveys to your child that you love him enough to spare your time and listen to him, and that you respect his person also. These will boost his self-esteem. A child learns to listen by you first listening to him and the earlier this habit is established, the closer your relationship will be with your child. Constantly ignoring your child when he wants to speak to you under any pretext will hamper your relationship with him in the long run. Listening is giving attention to your child; a child that is starved of this constantly disrupts adult conversation.

Listening could be passive or active. It is passive when you listen to fulfill all righteousness without taking serious what your child is saying. Active listening is your best gift to your child; focus your attention on your child while trying to understand his thoughts, feelings and expressions and reframing what he said in your own words to be sure you understood what he meant. Let your child confirm that you heard him properly. Active listening gives your child opportunity to reflect on the issue at hand as reframed by you; it improves his self-worth and self-respect because of the undivided attention he receives. This helps you to be empathetic to his cause and at the same time helps your child fill in any gap in your understanding of his plight.

In active listening, endeavor to hear what your child is saying and not what you expect to hear. Do not be distracted by the mode of delivery of what is being said rather focus on the content of what has been said. Listen with all your senses, pick up non-verbal cues and body languages and try to get what is left unsaid. Leave out exaggerations and focus on the message proper; and do not let your feelings interfere with the message you are getting. Pay attention to the emotion with which your child is speaking.

Listening to your child starts from the babyhood stage when a child's cry is the only way of communicating distress from hunger or wet diapers. Prompt attention brings relief to a child. Carry your baby and look at his face; when he coos or makes noise, respond with a smile or mimic his noise. Talk or read to your baby so that he can start recognizing your voice. At the toddler stage, the child has limited vocabulary; listen to whatever he is saying even when his grammar is wrong, allow him enough time to say what he has to say without displaying any impatience, answer his questions in simple language and assign a time to listening to him.

Adolescents need attention because of the numerous physiological and psychological changes taking place in their lives. Make out time for a one on one chat with your child regularly. Ask him open-ended questions such as "what activities did you engage in today?" Allow your child to have an opinion that is at variance with your thoughts on some issues. Respect his point of view. Do not lecture or criticize him because at this phase of life, a child could be very self conscious and can shut down if you severely criticize him. With teenagers, good communication will forestall needless arguments so foster it. Listen and try and appreciate his point of view, take an active interest in your child's life and let him know you are available for talks at his discretion.

Contrasting discipline with child physical abuse

Discipline is the practice of teaching and stimulating acceptable behavior in a child. It encompasses withdrawal of privileges, punishment to be served physically and creation of structured environment rules and boundaries. Discipline must be complimented by love to create balance and regulate the child's behavior. Different cultures have their own methods of discipline with an overall goal of producing order in society. The end result of discipline is acquisition of self-discipline and self-control in a child; these values are indispensable to living a productive life. Institutions like the military cherish discipline and place it at the core of all their activities. The British Royal Family aside from sending their children to very good schools like Oxford and Cambridge Universities, ensure that the male children served in the military. I believe the discipline of military life blends with royalty and sound education to give the children a well rounded life that will not bring reproach to the royal family.

Child abuse is deliberate infliction of injury on a child; it is not a corrective measure as opposed to discipline. It is often a recurrent habit that includes corporal punishment, neglect and emotional abuse. Physical abuse conveys to the child that he/she is unwanted. Child physical abuse is a reportable offense in developed countries and perpetrators of the act can be prosecuted and have their child taken away in extreme situations. Discipline makes a child respect boundaries and keep out of trouble. A disciplined child is law abiding. Child abuse on the other hand makes a child bitter, aggressive, rebellious and vengeful.

Discipline preserves life because it keeps a child out of danger while child abuse destroys the very essence of the child's person. Alcohol and substance abuse are consequences of lack of self control which abused children resort to in order to soothe their emotional pains. Self control protects disciplined children from all the social maladies of this age such as alcohol/substance abuse, teenage sex, teenage pregnancy, dropping out of school, gangsterism and gambling. Discipline is applied out of a sense of love and duty while child abuse is borne out of hate and frustration.

Discipline leads to a fruitful life because nothing worthwhile can be achieved without it. Child abuse, unless its effects are mitigated can lead to school dropout and an abused child may resort to a self-destructive lifestyle. Self-discipline and self-control which are the end products of discipline enable the child have good self-esteem necessary for a balanced life. Physically abused children have low self-esteem which makes them low achievers in life. Discipline never leaves a physical mark or emotional wounds on a child while physical abuse leaves physical scars and deep emotional wounds in a child for life. The pains of discipline last for a brief moment and bring about a harvest of noble works later in the child's life. The pains of child abuse are long lasting and could extend to the next generation.

Raising a child with choleric temperament

Choleric temperament is one of the four main temperaments a child is born with. It is easily the most unruly of all the temperaments. A child with a choleric temperament is full of energy, full of determination, decisive, and strong-willed. He is quick to make decisions and very often his decisions are sound and practicable; he does not shy away from providing leadership when an occasion demands it. He is quick to recognize opportunities and to capitalize on them. He very often succeeds where others have failed. His weaknesses are disdain for details, lack of compassion in his personal dealings; he is aggressive and unpredictable with a quick temper. He suffers fools gladly and could be very defensive and stubborn. He also has a tendency to run others down.

As early as age 5, a child with this temperament can keep you on your toes trying to boss you around. An older gentler sibling could be cowered into submitting to this budding tyrant. You should give such a child enough responsibilities at home to absorb his energy and prevent his intrusion into the lives of other members of the family. Deny him authority and control that do not belong to him in the home so that he will learn to obey constituted authority when outside the home.

Career-wise, most children with this temperament have the spirit of enterprise and this drives them to become entrepreneurs. Children with choleric temperament do well as coaches and as law enforcement officers. In raising a child with this temperament, the negative elements in him must be tempered. Such a child must be raised to develop empathy and patience for persons who are not as endowed as himself. Very early in life, he must be made to channel his energy into useful things such as sports or music. He needs social skills that would enable him to work in a team. Let him choose hobbies that are exciting to him. It is helpful to shield him from provocative situations that would easily snowball into a fight. Anger or distress is a trigger for them to escalate, so the firmer, calmer, and more decisive you are in calling them to order, the better for them.

He must be made accountable for his actions. Get him to keep to rules so that he will abide by the rule of the law and not end up a felon. He should be taught courtesy and consideration for others. He must develop emotional intelligence so as to be able to relate well with other persons.

Raising a child with a sanguine temperament

A child with a sanguine temperament is friendly, sociable, happy-go-lucky fellow who gets on with everyone in the family. He is hilarious and enjoys meeting new persons. He is full of enthusiasm and adapts to new situations easily. He makes promises at the drop of a pin but can hardly be relied on to keep them. You hear him before you see him, likes touching people while talking to them; he enjoys the company of people and is easily the social glue of his class. His energy makes him look more confident than he actually is; he can start a project and abandon it midway.

His weakness lies in his lack of discipline; he is prone to moral failure because he may not draw boundaries in his relationship with the opposite sex. He is weak in self-control and this might lead him to overeating and other excesses. He is very emotional and can cry as easily as he can fly into rage. He is very untidy in his person and in his room.

In raising a sanguine child, always hold him to his word so that he will not make frivolous promises. Control his restiveness by keeping him busy. Teach him responsibility by committing tasks into his hands. Teach him to learn to go over his homework so as to learn thoroughness and persistence. Teach him modesty in what he says and how he behaves so that he will not be boastful. Teach him to reflect on the morality of what he is about to do at all times so as to prevent moral failures in his life. Giving him various tasks to teach him commitment will help in stabilizing him.

Raising a child with a melancholic temperament

A child with a melancholic temperament is gentle, shy, timid, indecisive, cries easily, afraid of strangers and new environments. He is very sensitive to the comments of people, compassionate, diligent, conscientious, and has perfectionist tendencies. He is liable to moodiness and depression and does not make friends easily but when he does, he is dependable. He is very organized but overly analytical and critical of others. If his secondary temperament is phlegmatic, he will be outgoing.

A child with a melancholic temperament may grow up to choose a profession like medicine or be a scientist because of the sacrificial nature of the job. He can be legalistic and rigid, intolerant of people with opposing views. He must be trained to be an optimist, to have positive attitude to life and also learn positive self-talk to make it easy for people to associate with him. He could be meticulous to a fault.

In raising such a child, his weaknesses must be attended to; he must be taught good social skills. He will need a peer group where he receives positive attention and engages in an activity where he gets positive feedback. An activity like taekwondo or karate will boost his self-confidence. He should be engaged in volunteer activities that would make him focus his attention outwardly. Praise for successful accomplishments would boost his confidence. He should avoid joining competitive groups that will make him more critical of others. His environment such as school or neighborhood should not be changed unnecessarily so as not to destabilize him. Helping him get rid of irrational fears will go a long way in making him happy.

Raising a child with a phlegmatic temperament

A child with a phlegmatic temperament is calm, strong, balanced and unflappable; he is never in a hurry. He takes his time for whatever he has to do, hardworking and persistent. He is slow to make decisions and can be stubborn; he could be loyal to a fault. He loves the status quo and finds it hard to start out on a project but once he starts it, he sees it through to completion. He never volunteers for a new task but if he is assigned one, he acquits himself with distinction. Of all the temperaments, his is the easiest to get along with and the most timid also. He loves to observe others work without himself being engaged.

The phlegmatic can have a temper; he can endure provocation but when he explodes, people around will need to take cover. People with phlegmatic temperament make good teachers, counselors and administrators. They are very dependable and organized and make good group leaders. The phlegmatic's weakness lies in his lack of motivation, laziness, lack of drive and ambition. He is not internally motivated; he could be self-protective and selfish. Beneath his mild manners could be a stubborn person though he is also very fearful. He has a strong instinct for order and can be neat on his person.

While raising him, give him enough time for whatever you want him to do. Teach him how to allocate time to finish assigned task. He needs approval to build his self-confidence. You will need to teach him how to use his initiative to solve problems. Help him develop his emotional intelligence especially how to express emotions.

The problem of non-resident fathers

It takes two resident parents to raise normal, healthy and well behaved children; however the reality of divorce and its disruptive effect on family has made this ideal in many homes unattainable. Currently, more than 27 million children [39% of all US children] live apart from their father, and in a typical year, well over one third of these children won't even see their dads. Different countries have the problem of non-resident fathers to different degrees but the effect on the children remains the same unless measures are taken to mitigate these effects. More than half of all European-American children and three quarters of all African American children born since 1975 will live some part of their formative years with only one parent and in the vast majority of these cases; it is the father who will be absent.

Several researches attest to the effects of father-absence on children. Studies have shown that children with little or no contact with their fathers are more likely to drop out of school than those with resident fathers. Such children are more likely to involve in drug and alcohol abuse; the girls are more likely to become pregnant as teens while boys are more likely to become involved in crime and violence. While father-absence is not the only contributing factor to these kind of social problems, its role cannot be ignored because fathers play a key role in successful socialization of children. Unfortunately, there are instances when a father may be physically present in a home but may be emotionally disconnected from the children and so has no influence over them.

Educational achievement, self-esteem, responsible social behavior and adjustment to adult life are more noticeable in children who live with both parents. The major effect of father-absence is lessened parental attention because the single parent has to do the work of both parents. The intellectual achievement of the child is reduced while general behavioral problems such as aggression in male children may arise. Father-absence is also associated with economic downtown in the family; research has found that over 65% of children living with never married mothers are living below the poverty line as against 10% of children living in two-parent homes. Children of fathers who pay child support do better in school and have fewer behavioral problems than children whose fathers do not pay child support. Helping with homework when a non-resident father is around, setting and enforcing rules of behavior for the child and supervising the child all help in producing better behaved children.

Staying connected to your child for life

Many children lose connection with their parents after school, marriage and getting a job in a city far from where their parents live. Some children manage to keep in touch while others have very little to do with their parents other than occasional visits or phone calls to them. This is particularly true in situations where the child did not grow up under the same roof with the parent. The labor of raising children cannot be quantified and if there are no quarrels between children and parents, today's world has enough gadgets to enable parents to stay connected to their children. Children who have significantly more positive interactions with their parents than negative interactions are more likely to stay connected for life.

Communication is vital for staying connected. This could be through phone calls, text messages, Skype, electronic and snail mail. Pictures at the work place and of grandchildren convey to parents love and appreciation for the role they played in their child's life. Visits should be made to parents not just when they are ill but at different times of the year to keep them company and also to make the grandchildren thrill them. Visits afford a child the opportunity to find out if the parents are in need of anything. Inviting parents to spend time with their child also helps them stay connected. Visits enable a parent communicate his/her expectations to the child.

Parents should not be controlling in dealing with their children; allow them to learn the ropes of building their families. Unsolicited advice may be unhelpful but when asked for, give it. Unnecessary intrusion into the family life of your children may cause bad blood between you and your child. Be interested in the progress of your children and celebrate their achievements; this makes you a part of their support system. If there are shared interests between parent and child; for example if both are writers, there is an interface for continuous interaction between them. They can proof read each other's writing and do a critique for one another.

Always acknowledge the care your child gives you and do not be shy to ask for support and solace if the need arises. Pray for your children that it would be well with them and their families.

Striking a balance between work and family life

So many homes have disintegrated because of the inability to strike the balance between work and family life. This has left many children distraught from resulting divorce. Children have limited time to spend at home, so parents must make time available to foster necessary values in them. Parents also need time themselves to unwind and have fun to keep their sanity. The work place situation is desperate because employees have more work due to downsizing and outsourcing of jobs while managers can call you up anytime for new developments at work. Therefore, an employee has to work harder to keep his job. How can parents strike this balance between work and family in an ever busy world?

A parent should acknowledge his/her limitations and the challenges on hand pertaining to work. He/she needs a good family life to sustain his/her success at work in same way; he/she needs the job to finance the family. This calls for time budgeting. What can be done at home to impact the family positively before and after work? Activities before work may include family devotion and having breakfast together; after work activities could be involvement in guiding and monitoring children at their homework as well as having supper together. This however, would depend on when parents get home. Take time to nurture your relationships. They are a pillar in your life.

Giving attention to personal wellbeing is also very important. Activities like physical exercise, ensuring good nutrition, rest and adequate sleep replenish energy. Emotional life and spiritual life must be nurtured to avoid falling apart as a person. Indulge yourself regularly everyday in a hobby or whatever gives you clean fun. This goes a long way in relieving stress. This personal time which may be as little as 15 minutes daily should be considered sacrosanct. It is your share of the day which should be focused on your person. Your private time should be considered an engagement with your person. Take time to nurture your relationship with yourself. Without this you could feel boxed in.

Restricting work to the work place and not bringing work home is a good habit that takes effort to nurture. Use your time of commuting to work to switch from home to work mode and on your way home switch back to the home mode. Do not feel guilty about creating a dichotomy between work time and family time; you might have to turn off your phone and computer to actualize this. Your work place is designed to squeeze out all the time and energy you can give to your company so internally resist sharing home time with your work. .When you give the impression that you can accommodate more tasks during your work time, more work will be assigned you. Instead, let your goal be to take on less work; however aim at personal fulfillment in your schedule lest your work becomes drudgery. Overwork causes negative emotions that affect the whole family and your relationships. Studies have shown that tired workers are less productive, have higher healthcare costs and are more prone to workplace accidents. Work and family life imbalance is associated with fatigue, lost time with loved ones and friends and more jobs from the workplace because of increased expectations.

A mother should take maternal leave even if it impacts negatively on her career. The benefit of raising a well groomed child outweighs the career benefits. One should be ready to pay a price for what one believes in. At work, manage your time well, delegate duties or dispense with activities that are unimportant. Take advantage of your work options such as job sharing, telecommuting and scheduling flexibility. Practice assertiveness by saying "no" respectfully when you are called to take on more tasks. Do not give room for feelings of guilt or a false sense of obligation for rejecting tasks that are not yours; this attitude will give you more time for worthwhile activities. At home use daily to-do list and rank activities in order of importance, put family events on weekly calendar so as not to forget them. Have group activities involving your family members and friends. This helps to nurture your relationships while serving as a form of relaxation. Developing a network of friends at work who can stand in the gap for you when there are family exigencies is a good idea; having another set of friends at home who can help with your family responsibilities when you work overtime is wisdom. You must learn to accept things not done to your satisfaction if only to reduce stress and maintain sanity.

It is good to seek professional help from a counselor when you are not coping. Work and family interests will evolve and keep increasing as you climb your career ladder and as your children grow. If you managed to lay a solid foundation before commitments increase at both ends, you will have a good reference point to remediate your situation.

Managing stress related to parenting

Parenting under normal circumstances is accompanied by some measure of stress because different stages of a child's life have different demands. When the number of children is large, the stress is multiplied. Caring for small children is physically demanding because the children are totally dependent on their parents for care. Caring for adolescents and teenagers has its own share of stress because they spend a lot of time out of the home. Children with special needs put a lot of stress on parents because of the special attention they need. Single parents do the work of two so the pressure is double on them and for two parents with full time jobs, they do not have time for family social activities, hobbies or interests because of raising their children. It is important to have a realistic attitude that your children will be children and will grow up to be normal children. To be worried if they are getting all the care they need every moment simply drains life from you.

Recognizing stress signs early so as to forestall adverse effects on your health as well as enable you to take stress reduction measures is very important. Stress manifests as fatigue, being irritable over small matters, sleeplessness or non-refreshing sleep, headaches, poor concentration, feeling pressured, impatience, forgetfulness, anger and anxiety. Juggling career with parenting produces stress; admit this and think of what to do. To cope with stress, you must understand where it is coming from, recognize the symptoms of excessive stress and make necessary adjustments to reduce stress. You minimize stress when you are realistic and you stop trying to be a perfect parent. You realize that since children are different, what works with one child may not work with another. Be prepared for the unexpected at all times instead of being shocked by every new development. Practice time management by drawing up a to-do list which prioritizes your commitments. Ask for help when you need it especially if you are a single parent.

Fifteen minutes of time for yourself everyday for personal activities like meditation, daily devotion, good nutrition, recreation and physical exercise will reduce your stress. Ensure you have good sleep to replenish your energy. Give yourself a break from looking after your children; either get someone to look after them while you take out time to do something pleasurable or attend to a pressing need. Parental stress can lead to depression or other mental problems if not handled properly. When under stress, do not take it out on your family otherwise a deep sense of guilt will come upon you. Utilize babysitting facilities in your neighborhood and attend community programs for parents and children that teach better coping skills while affording you an opportunity to interact with other parents from whom you may get some ideas to cope better. Joining a parenting support group has a lot of advantages especially getting to know that other parents are facing similar challenges. Building good relationships has stress reducing advantages especially knowing that you have a listening ear when you are under stress.